IMAGES
of America

FRANKLIN TOWNSHIP,
HUNTERDON COUNTY

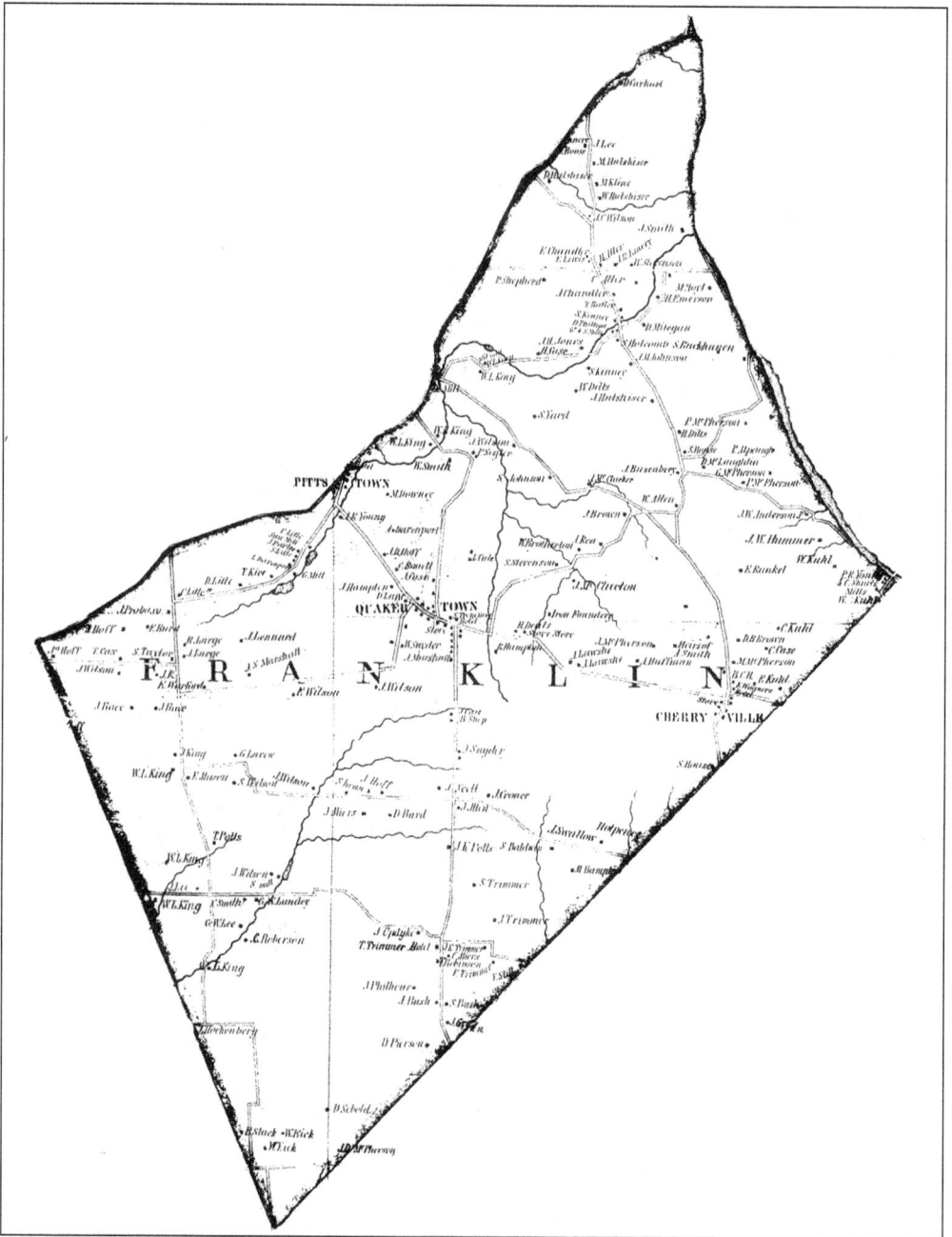

This map of Franklin Township by Samuel C. Cornell was published in 1851 by Lloyd Van Derveer and S. C. Cornell. (Courtesy Hunterdon County Historical Society.)

ON THE COVER: In this typical scene from about 1910 in rural Franklin, Brevoort W. Conover (left) and Newt Trimmer (right) are in the front wagon, and Sam Gano (back, left) and friends follow. Coming up the hill from Pittstown after delivering milk, the men are leaning on full sacks of grain, most likely purchased at the Pittstown Mill. The Conover farm was located halfway between Pittstown and Quakertown. (Courtesy Virginia and Brevoort C. Conover.)

IMAGES
of America

FRANKLIN TOWNSHIP, HUNTERDON COUNTY

Dan and Marty Campanelli and Lora Jones
for Rural Awareness, Inc.

ARCADIA
PUBLISHING

Published by Arcadia Publishing
Charleston SC, Chicago IL, Portsmouth NH, San Francisco CA

Library of Congress Control Number:2009931546

For all general information contact Arcadia Publishing at:
Telephone 843-853-2070
Fax 843-853-0044
E-mail sales@arcadiapublishing.com
For customer service and orders:
Toll-Free 1-888-313-2665

Visit us on the Internet at www.arcadiapublishing.com

James Passerello hugs his pet Lamikens in 1954 on the farm purchased by his grandparents Theodore and Grace Peters, when his mother, Frances, was just a few months old. Now all grown up, he has restored the c. 1780 stone house, preserved the land, and continues to farm with his wife, the former Mary Timko. (Courtesy James and Mary Passerello and Judith Winfield.)

CONTENTS

ACKNOWLEDGMENTS

When this project was started, a request for vintage photographs was printed in the township newsletter and area newspapers. The first to respond and to share his family pictures was Brevoort C. Conover, who grew up just outside Quakertown on a farm established by his grandfather, who appears on the cover. Conover also called several family members and interest grew. Residents told cousins who had moved away, and neighbors talked to neighbors.

Nearly 2,000 photographs were viewed, and several hundred were scanned for the Franklin Archives, where it is hoped they will be used for other historical publications in the future. Boy Scout Troop 108, the Franklin Archives, the Hunterdon County Historical Society, the *Hunterdon Democrat*, Quakertown Friends Meeting, and 46 families supplied the 220 images included in the book. Each is credited in the captions. Since there are several group photographs—even one with 450 people—more than 46 families are represented.

We owe a debt of gratitude to Willis W. Vail (1868–1951) for documenting community events daily in both words and pictures over the 63 years from 1887 to 1950. Images from several of his glass-plate negatives are included here, and quotes from his diary are sprinkled throughout the captions.

Thanks are due as well to J. Edward Stout (1923–2001), who served as Franklin historian for 19 years and rescued Vail's diaries for the Franklin Archives. His township history, *Facts and Fantasies of Franklin*, provided great help in solving some historical mysteries.

Erin Rocha, our editor, was a joy to work with, responding immediately to our questions. Arcadia Publishing provides a great service to history through its Images of America series. We believe without their interest, many family pictures like those in this book would be lost as generations pass. For that, we are deeply grateful. We also are grateful for the people we met and the family stories we heard about life in Franklin in days gone by. We are all better for it.

INTRODUCTION

By the time European settlers entered the area now known as Franklin Township in Hunterdon County, Native Americans had already occupied the land for at least 5,000 years. Known as Lenape Indians, they were hunters, fishermen, and gatherers who also gardened and practiced horticulture in their semipermanent and sometimes permanent villages. Many of the artifacts they left behind, such as stone arrowheads, adzes, gouges, and mortar stones, are still discovered and treasured by local residents.

In 1676, the English colony of New Jersey was divided into East Jersey and West Jersey. By 1680, Quaker proprietors, including William Penn, were granted the right to govern this western tract. From that time, land here was purchased from the local Native Americans and divided up into smaller tracts. Named Hunterdon for Royal Gov. Robert Hunter, this county was set off from Burlington County by an act of the general assembly on March 11, 1713.

The township of Bethlehem was founded in 1730, and Kingwood was split off in 1749. From Kingwood, Franklin was hived off in 1845. Franklin's villages and hamlets were known by different names at earlier times, including Quakertown, Pittstown, Cherryville, Kingtown, Landsdown, Sidney, Littletown, Oak Grove, and Grandin.

The first settlers to reach what is now Franklin Township came soon after 1700 and were Quakers from Burlington. These Friends chose the vicinity around Quakertown because of its idyllic rolling hills, fine creeks, rich soils, and absence of woods, since the Lenape Indians had kept much of the land burned off for hunting grounds. The Friends' original c. 1733 meetinghouse was built of logs; a stone one replaced it in 1747.

The first pioneer structures were usually hewn of local oak and chestnut and had large fieldstone fireplaces for cooking and heating. With growing families, these buildings were eventually replaced with stone structures of one or two rooms and a sleeping loft above. Stone lean-to additions were usually placed on the chimney gable end to cover their bread ovens and to keep wood dry. Around the last half of the 1700s, larger English-style stone or braced-frame clapboard structures were being added on to the earlier buildings. Two interesting building features found in Franklin were back-to-back corner fireplaces and a unique mortise-and-tenon joint for floor joists known as "bird's tongue."

During the Revolutionary War, many patriots graced the villages of Franklin. Two notable ones are worth mentioning. Moore Furman, deputy quartermaster general of New Jersey lived in Pittstown during the war, and in 1778, he built a stone gristmill to supply flour and bread for Gen. George Washington's army. Furman later established a nail factory, a distillery, a general store, a hotel, and several dwelling houses. Charles Stewart of Landsdown was appointed colonel of Hunterdon's first regiment of minutemen in 1775, as well as commissary general of issues from 1777 to 1783.

It has been written in old local history books that during the war, the Quaker meetinghouse was "used and abused," and a Quaker named John Allen had his home and land confiscated by wintering British troops. New research in 2005, using Quaker meeting notes, a revolutionary pension claim, maps, and more, shows the old story was confused. No British troops were in Quakertown; however, Allen was imprisoned by Continental troops in 1778 for not signing an oath of allegiance to the State of New Jersey, since Quakers could not sign oaths.

Many outstanding people shaped the communities of Franklin. They cannot all be listed, but three must be recognized. John Deats patented the Deats plow in 1828. In 1831, his son Hiram started a small iron industry of farm machinery, which thrived first in Quakertown, then in Pittstown, and was ended in the early 1900s. Beloved citizen Willis W. Vail was born in 1868 in Quakertown. Quaker and caretaker of the old meetinghouse, Vail also was township treasurer, on the board of education, and started Troop 108 as the first Boy Scout leader. His hobby was photography and many of his pictures grace this book, as well as his written observations.

Franklin's first schools in the 1700s were small log cabins. They were poorly heated and had little light or creature comforts. In the early 1800s, they were replaced with stone structures. By 1850, a two-story stone building was erected in Quakertown as a private academy and later became a public school. Communities such as Cherryville, Pittstown, Quakertown, and Sidney built their own schools, and by 1879, there were five frame schoolhouses (two around Quakertown) with a total of 273 pupils. In 1937, all the one-room schoolhouses were replaced with the new Franklin Township Consolidated School in Quakertown.

Township churches included the early Friends meetinghouse, the 1850 Baptist church in Cherryville, the 1879 Quakertown United Methodist Church, and the 1896 Calvary-Brethren Church near Croton (no longer in use). Three churches were added more recently: the 1967 South Ridge Community Church, the 1992 St. Catherine of Siena Catholic Church, and the 1993 Wesleyan Faith Chapel.

Agriculture was the first and most important industry. Early crops were buckwheat, rye, and flax, and later wheat, maize, and oats were grown. Farmers grew a variety of vegetables and fruits and kept all types of livestock. They often had a second occupation like shoemaking, carpentry, leather working, masonry, blacksmithing, or furniture making.

Before the mid-1800s, individual villages had evolved into self-sufficient towns, with hotels, post offices, general stores, taverns, and an array of specialty businesses.

Two sources of waterpower important to early settlers were the Capoolong Creek, which empties into the South Branch of the Raritan River, and the Lockatong Creek, which starts below Quakertown and flows to the Delaware River. An early industry was mills for grist, fulling, oil, wool-carding, weaving, and wood cutting. Transporting produce out of the area was done the hard way by horse and wagon until 1872, when the Easton and Amboy Railroad was extended to Landsdown, and in 1891, when the Lehigh Valley Railroad was opened to Pittstown. The newfangled automobile entered the scene around 1900, doing about 15 miles per hour.

An act establishing the Township of Franklin was approved on March 21, 1845, and the first town meeting was held in April of that year. A telephone company was incorporated in 1910, and electric service came to rural Franklin in the 1920s, relying on old gristmills to produce the power. The Quakertown Fire Company, founded in 1914, was reorganized in 1951. The Quakertown Volunteer Emergency Medical Service was founded in 1989. Since the township's inception, constables kept law and order, but the official police department was established in 1967.

Franklin residents served in every war since the American Revolution, many giving their lives to maintain the freedoms enjoyed here today. While the earliest occupants were mostly of English ancestry, the township started to see an influx of middle-European families by the late 1800s. Their cultivation of the land has been an asset to the community. Today citizens still enjoy the historic villages and the beautiful 14,746 acres of rolling hills and green farm fields, with more than 3,226 acres of the township permanently preserved for farmland or recreation.

It has been just over 300 years since the first settlers came to the area known today as Franklin Township in Hunterdon County.

One

VILLAGES AND HAMLETS

Maple Glen Farm near Cherryville, shown around 1890, was established in 1874 by William B. Volk. It has been home to five generations of Volks, four of which have served on Franklin's board of education. Fifth-generation member Laura Zell Volk Zimmerman helps Franklin preserve open space and farmland. The house was moved from this site a quarter of a mile closer to Cherryville Road in the 1970s. (Courtesy Volk family.)

The center stone section of the Pittstown Mill was built in 1778 by New Jersey deputy quartermaster general of provisions Moore Furman. The mill produced flour to feed Gen. George Washington's army at encampments throughout the state. This old postcard shows later additions to the mill. The Bodine family ran a feed, lumber, and paint company there from 1897 to 1981. This local landmark still stands today. (Courtesy George and Sandra Baker.)

Pittstown was named in honor of William Pitt, Earl of Chatham, who was a supporter of the American cause. The village was virtually self-sufficient, with businesses such as a general store, post office, tavern, blacksmith, and more. Here Peter A. Hann poses outside of his barbershop on Main Street around 1930. Hann and his wife, Katie, lived across the road in a stucco-over-stone Colonial home. (Courtesy Joan Mathews.)

Traditionally this high road overlooking Main Street in Pittstown was home to the village's most affluent families. In the late 1800s, many of the houses were Victorianized. Utility poles at right help date this real-photo postcard. The Franklin Telephone Company was incorporated in 1910, and electricity came to the area in the 1920s, largely because of the efforts of Dr. Morris Leaver and Willis W. Vail, two prominent citizens. (Courtesy Franklin Archives.)

Dalrymple's Store, near the Pittstown Mill, housed gasoline pumps and the village post office in this late-1940s scene. This was a place for people to gather and exchange news and gossip. Today Perricone's Market continues the tradition with a family-run enterprise in the same building. West of the store and out of view lies a lower area with the old train depot and former manufacturing operations. (Courtesy George and Sandra Baker.)

11

This view from the southeast shows the farm fields and fences behind Main Street in Quakertown. It was photographed by Willis W. Vail on November 29, 1894, as a glass-plate negative. At far left is the old Friends meetinghouse, and at far right is the Quakertown United Methodist Church. Dwellings and shops fill in the spaces between these two religious icons of the village. (Courtesy Hunterdon County Historical Society.)

Franklin House Hotel, pictured around 1910, was established as a tavern in 1767 by Daniel Cahill, one of Quakertown's first innkeepers. Samuel Trimmer ran it in 1845, when it was the site of the first Franklin Township Committee meeting. Trimmer served as village postmaster from 1857 to 1869; the hotel remained active until 1919. The porch was removed around 1945 when the county widened the road. (Courtesy Franklin Archives.)

Snow obscures Croton Road at its intersection with Quakertown Road (the main street) around 1940 in a scene that looks much the same today. The view is toward Croton Road past frame houses and the Quakertown United Methodist Church, all built between 1860 and 1885 and all listed in the State and National Register of Historical Places. The cluster of buildings served to expand the village southward. (Courtesy Mary Bodine and family.)

The corner store in Quakertown was built in 1844 by G. W. Waterhouse at the intersection of Croton Road, helping to anchor the side street to the village. It offered general merchandise and, over time, had several owners. This picture from the second decade of the 20th century was taken when George E. Race ran the store. Regardless of the owner, the porch was always a popular gathering place for catching up on local news. (Courtesy Franklin Archives.)

Benjamin and Phoebe Coddington built a stone cottage on their Quakertown farm around 1765 and sold the property to Peter Potter in 1772. John Allen purchased the farm in 1776 and added a two-story stone addition in the 1790s. Willis W. Vail, Allen's great-great-grandson, took this picture in 1925, two years after enlarging the original cottage. The property remained with Allen descendants until Vail sold it in 1934. (Courtesy Dan and Marty Campanelli.)

Vail found this rare, tanbark millstone buried along the stream on his farm in 1926. First Peter Potter then Allen had a tanning business there in the late 1700s. This scallop-edged millstone was used upright and turned by oxen to crush tree bark, which contained tannins used to soften leather. The millstone now stands in front of the old homestead. (Photograph by Marty Campanelli.)

A 1795 survey map shows a two-story log cabin at the intersection of Main Street and Croton Road in Quakertown. However, the present clapboard structure was built prior to 1850 and occupied by Abraham Lawshe. Lawshe was on the first town committee in 1845 when Franklin was hived off from Kingwood Township. George and Nancy Race owned the property and the general store across the road when this photograph was taken in 1934. (Courtesy Droppa family.)

This late-1800s clapboard house across from the Quakertown United Methodist Church was purchased in 1935 by Willis W. and Belle Gough Vail. Former township historian J. Edward Stout acquired Willis's diaries, photographs, and numerous glass-plate negatives at the Vails's estate auction around 1960. The Aller family was next to occupy the residence, and their grandson George found more glass-plate negatives in 1970. Some are included in this book. (Courtesy Aller family.)

This stone-and-frame dwelling on Quaker Lane in Quakertown dates to the late 1700s. It is known locally as the Still House Farm because when John Trimmer Jr. bought it in 1873, he built a cider mill and distillery on the property. Both are now gone. This photograph from the early 1940s does not show later additions. Today it is a two-family dwelling. (Courtesy Kenneth and Margaret Shepperd.)

John Harned and Mary Willson Vail turned an earlier Quakertown structure into an Italianate-style dwelling in 1867. John owned and ran the general store next door until 1895 and was postmaster on and off for 19 years. The Vails and their children, Willis, Evangeline, and James, were active members of the Friends meetinghouse. Willis took this back view of their home in 1891. (Courtesy Aller family.)

16

In 1749, Irish immigrant Thomas Little bought 100 acres to establish a homestead (below). This structure, built as a gristmill, was called Little's Mill. In the 1880s, Emley H. Deats, Hiram's grandson, made it a sawmill, a peach basket factory, and then added a steam engine to make roller buckwheat flour. The site has since been called Deats Castle. Today it is a private dwelling. (Courtesy Ella M. Haver.)

Dorothy Crist White, with son Richard Joseph, lived in the Little family farmstead on Pittstown Road during World War II. Her daughter Irma remembers their victory garden. The stone house was built in the last half of the 1700s to replace a 1749 one-room log cabin built by Irish immigrants Thomas Little and Esther Christy. Because several family descendants settled in the area, locals call it Littletown. (Courtesy Irma White Parsons.)

This 1907 postcard shows the southwest corner of the crossroads in Cherryville, a hamlet established in 1839. By 1881, it had a post office, a church, a store, wheelwright and blacksmith shops, and a dozen homes. It is much the same today but without commerce. The c. 1820 building at left housed blacksmith John A. Swarer's shop from 1887 to 1926. It was a lace mill in the 1930s and is now a storage shed. (Courtesy Franklin Archives.)

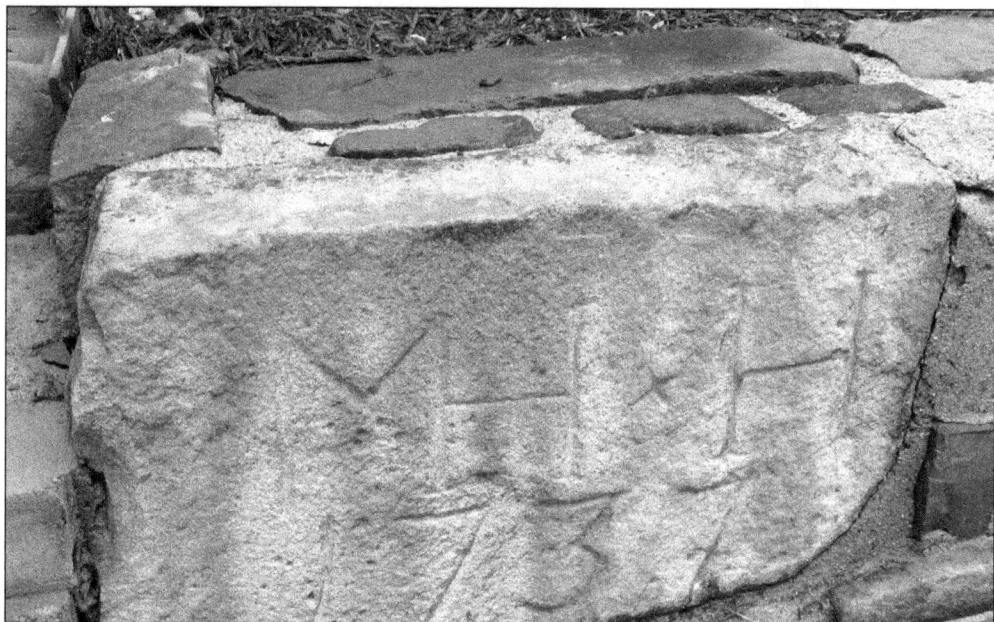

The 1881 *History of Hunterdon County* by James P. Snell cited the tavern-house in Cherryville "built in 1739" as "the oldest landmark in that vicinity." Recent repairs to the tavern, he wrote, concealed its date stone. Originally called the Dogtown Tavern, the building grew into the Cherryville Inn. When it burned on February 14, 1952, the true date on the stone was revealed as 1737. (Photograph by Marty Campanelli.)

18

This house on the south edge of Cherryville had its origins in 1762 as one room with a walk-in fireplace and sleeping loft. Sometime in the 1880s, the residing family, headed by Cherryville district clerk Samuel Chamberlain McPherson, posed for an Allentown, Pennsylvania, photographer. From left to right are Samuel; his wife, Mary Ann; daughter Lucretia; son Bergen; and daughter Elmira. (Courtesy H. James and Katherine E. Griffith.)

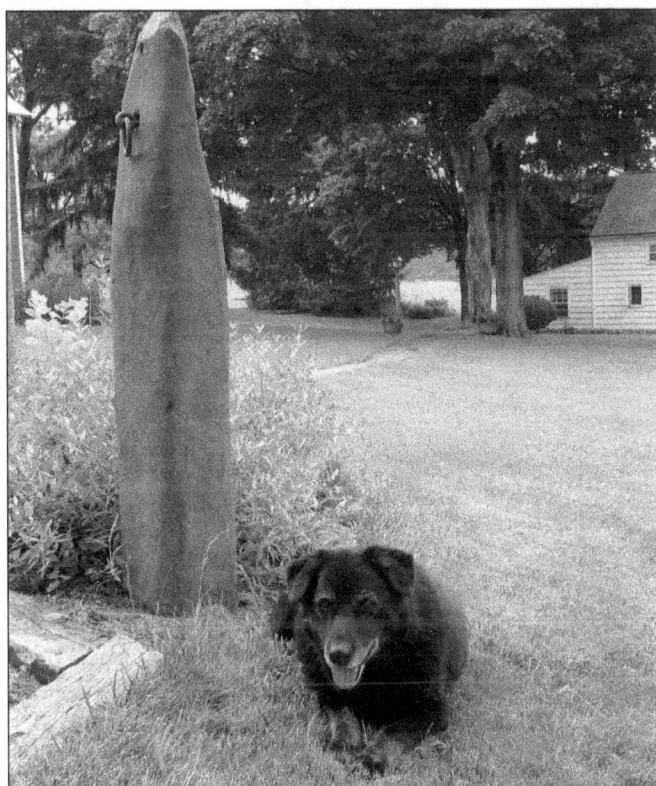

This blue jingle stone hitching post, originally at the Cherryville Inn, now stands at a preserved farm nearby. Fred Polacsek, whose grandparents owned the inn from 1925 to the 1940s, saved the stone from encroaching modern roads after the inn burned. He remembers hanging from the post's iron ring to "swing my legs back and forth . . . a form of recreation for little folks in the 20s." (Photograph by Marty Campanelli.)

In 1915, Grace Martin Peters (center) and her husband, Theodore Bernhard Peters (right), posed with who is believed to be Jeramiah Roberson, their landlord at the stone house at Allens Corner and Croton Roads. The newlywed Peters were renting and shopping for a farm. They settled on 70 acres on Quakertown Road in 1918, starting a three-generation succession of family members on the land. (Courtesy James and Mary Passerello and Judith Winfield.)

This property, seen in the late 1950s, is at the corner of Croton and Franklin School Roads diagonally across from the house above. Its history dates to 1730 when Jacob Doughty sold 260 acres and a tenant building to John Coat. The mid-1700s house, carriage house, and 1879 main barn exist today. Current residents have restored the buildings and added gardens, orchards, and 50 alpacas. (Courtesy Tim and Sandy Maxwell.)

Visiting neighbors has always been a popular recreational choice in rural Franklin. In 1920, the Aller family of Upper Kingtown Road, one of Franklin's scenic rural roads, documented the visit of their neighbors, the Stetlers. From left to right are Mr. Stetler, George Aller behind his son James, Aller's daughter Grace partially hiding her sister Elizabeth, Mrs. Stetler, Naomi Aller (George's wife), and son Nathan Aller in front of her. (Courtesy Aller family.)

Taverns were among Franklin's first businesses. Here Theresa and Ambrose Gansfuss stand behind the counter in the original Chicken Coop Tavern built about 1945. Their son Eugene sits at the left with an unidentified couple. In 1946, the tavern got Franklin's first television set. In 1948, the business was relocated from near Sidney Brook to its current location in Sidney. In 1980, the Clinton Elks Lodge No. 2434 assumed its management. (Courtesy Eugene Gansfuss.)

This large stone house in Landsdown was built by Col. Charles Stewart in 1761 on land given to him by his father-in-law Judge Samuel Johnson. Stewart was a colonel of New Jersey's first regiment of minutemen, a member of the first provincial congress of New Jersey, and commissary general of issue during the American Revolution. The property has had numerous owners and gone through many changes and additions. (Courtesy Aller family.)

This 1850s structure in Sunnyside, shown around 1960, was originally the blacksmith and wheelwright shop of Edward Bloom. In 1931, Samuel Stothoff, founder of a well-drilling company, bought the property and converted the shop into a dwelling for his daughter Florence and her husband, J. Edward Crowl, a land surveyor. Stothoff's grandson Peter and his family now occupy it. Note the millstone in the chimney. (Courtesy Peter J. Crowl family.)

On the same day in 1894 that Willis W. Vail photographed the Stewart house in Landsdown, he took a picture of this stone dwelling a mile down the road towards Sidney. Originally built in the 1730s by Col. Daniel Coxe, the 1,200-acre tract was sold to the chief magistrate of West Jersey Judge Samuel Johnson by 1740. Its next owners were the Wilsons, and then Coxe descendants bought the property back. The house was rebuilt by them after a fire in 1802. Two young boys can be seen peering from the doorway upon closer examination of Vail's photograph. The property was in the possession of the Kinney family from 1867 to 1898, so these cute tykes may well be family members. (Courtesy Hunterdon County Historical Society.)

Franklin has 183 frame houses that were built before 1900, like this large home shown in March 1935, when the 50-acre property was farmed by Hugo and Christina Jensen Leusenring. Today it sits on 20 acres dedicated to training young women in equestrian pursuits. As is typical in Franklin, the house commands beautiful views of a valley, lake, and blue-cast hills. (Courtesy Aller family.)

This dwelling, shown around 1954, is one of Franklin's 99 Colonial-era stone structures. It stands on land ceded to George Kline by King George III of England. The main section is said to date to the last third of the 18th century; the lower section was added in two stages in 1832 and 1852. The McPherson family held it for 124 years; only four other families have owned it since. (Courtesy Franklin Archives.)

Two

FACES OF FRANKLIN

Michael and Susanna Farr Tinnes, naturalized Americans from Romania, lived on what is now West Sidney Road. Five of their 12 children are shown at the wagon house where the family made tomato crates. The carriage house and "apple pie" tree are in the background. The children are, from left to right, Matthew Tinnes in Walter Tinnes's lap, visiting playmate Herb Tietjan, Edward Tinnes, William Tinnes, and Alvina Tinnes. (Courtesy Tinnes family.)

On a clear Sunday afternoon in 1894, Willis W. Vail "took a picture of the Leaver children." Morris Leaver, second from right, was a prominent physician and dentist in Franklin. Leaver poses with his wife, Cora, and his siblings. From left to right are Willie, Lucy in Cora's lap, Amy, Morris, and Albert. Note the bowler hat on the shrub and Willie's grin. (Courtesy Hunterdon County Historical Society.)

Vail noted on May 16, 1895, "Today is Abram and Jane Vail's golden wedding. Mother, Evangeline and I went. Fifty-six took dinner, I believe." The celebrants are seated at front center; Willis appears at the top left. Family names written on back of the photograph are still prominent in Franklin, including Vail, Alpaugh, Case, Gary, Gartley, Robinson, Trimmer, Trout, and Pound. (Courtesy Quakertown Friends Meeting.)

Well over a century after his death in 1887 at age 77, Hiram Deats is still remembered in Franklin Township for both his lifelong dedication to active citizenship and for his manufacture of agricultural equipment that won national recognition for the villages of Pittstown and Quakertown in the early 19th century. He also manufactured stoves, kettles, and school desks and became the county's first millionaire. A three-story brick building he erected in Flemington still stands at 122–124 Main Street. He was a founding member of the Cherryville Baptist Church and is buried in the cemetery there, as are many generations of his family. Deats married twice: Rebecca Higgins (1820–1862) of Hillsborough and Elmira Stevenson (1831–1908) of Illinois. His son from the second marriage, Hiram Edmond (1870–1963), became the leading authority on state and local history and one of the nation's preeminent philatelists. The Hunterdon County Historical Society's library is named in his honor. (Courtesy Hunterdon County Historical Society.)

The famous Deats plow was designed and patented in 1828 by Hiram Deats's father, John. It was advertised as scouring the earth better than any before it and withstanding great strain without breaking. An 1840s catalog lists several plows priced from $9 to $16. Customers said, "They are less liable to get out of order than other ploughs . . . they run without choking with rubbish." (Courtesy Hunterdon County Historical Society.)

These tintypes matted together in paper date to about 1860. They portray Elizabeth Case and her father, Christopher Case. Elizabeth married William B. Volk, who acquired land from his father-in-law and built the house on Maple Glen Farm near Cherryville. Elizabeth's sister married William's brother, an occurrence repeated in the Volk family three generations later. (Courtesy Volk family collection.)

John J. Volk, photographed around 1880, was born on March 17, 1859, and was part of the second generation of Volks on the farm. He married Laura Henry, who grew up a short distance down the road to Flemington, but her family's house no longer exists. The couple had three sons, but only two, William Marvin and John, survived. Continuing his father's tradition, John J. was active in the community. (Courtesy Volk family collection.)

Jennie M. Haver, shown dressed for her 1906 high school graduation, earned a master's degree in education from Rutgers University and in 1916 became the county and state's first helping teacher. Her work proved so beneficial that legislation was passed to adopt the system statewide. Widely admired, she was honored at her death in 1956 with a memorial fund that annually provides college scholarships to county students. (Courtesy Ella M. Haver.)

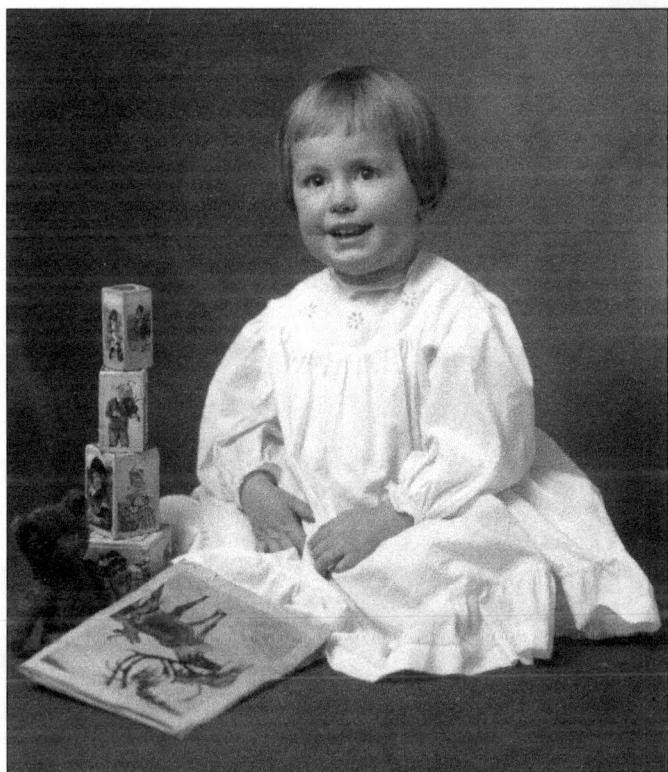

Ella M. Haver, seen at age two in 1915, is the niece of Jennie. Following in her aunt's footsteps, Ella started her career as a teacher in a one-room schoolhouse. She taught high school biology and chemistry for 40 years and has taught Sunday school classes for 80 years. In retirement, her primary focus is the administration of the Jennie M. Haver Memorial Scholarship Fund. (Courtesy Ella M. Haver.)

According to Willis W. Vail's diary, it was a fad around 1887 for Friends to dress in old-style clothing for photographs, like these five daughters, ages 20 to 39, of Abram and Jane Vail. From left to right are Lizzie D. Trimmer, Laura D. Trout, Rebecca H. Case, Clara V. Gary, and Adelia S. Robinson. It is believed that Elias Dalrymple took the picture. (Courtesy Quakertown Friends Meeting.)

Willis W. Vail photographed his father, John Harned Vail, and sister Evangeline in "Aunt Annie's" parlor on November 18, 1913, the day before Evangeline married Burris Snyder. After John sold his store in 1895 and lost his wife in 1900, he and Evangeline traveled between Oregon and Florida. Note the fancy stove and china-filled cabinet with a hornet's nest hanging from its top. (Courtesy Hunterdon County Historical Society.)

John D. Trout, seen here on his farm with his team of horses, worked at the general store owned by John Harned Vail in Quakertown. Vail sold the store in 1895, according to Willis's diary, to Josiah A. Trimmer and Trout. Trout also served as township tax collector from 1903 to 1910 and as Quakertown postmaster from 1915 until 1939. (Courtesy Janice Wene Haas.)

John Kuhl, born in 1828, lived his life as a farmer in the Cherryville area. He married Thisby Stevenson in 1857 and had two sons, Elisha and Christopher. Stevenson died in 1863, and several years later, Kuhl married Almeda Bartow. They had one son, Pierson, in 1873. Kuhl died of a stroke on January 1, 1894, and was described in his obituary as "thrifty, successful, pleasant, sociable and kind." (Courtesy John W. Kuhl.)

Guests one Sunday afternoon around 1897 at the Charles and Olive Burd farm are, from left to right, Maria Shepherd, unidentified young man against tree, Sarah Conover, Brevoort W. Conover, Henry Vanderbilt (partially hidden), Theodore Shepherd, possibly Abraham Shepherd, Charles (seated on ground), Olive (back to camera), Annie Vanderbilt, and Mary Shepherd. The baby at the rear may be Lloyd, the first son of Brevoort and Sarah. (Courtesy Virginia and Brevoort C. Conover.)

Lela Hanna (left) poses with her sister-in-law Elizabeth Hanna Shepperd and horses at Still House Farm in Quakertown. Elizabeth, a popular midwife in the 1920s, also was quite the horsewoman, regularly driving her horse and buggy with a folding top into Flemington 6 miles away. She was a perennial participant in parades there with her rig. (Courtesy Kenneth and Margaret Shepperd.)

James and Martha German settled on a large and productive farm near Cherryville and had four children, George, Elmer, Johnson, and Lillian. Four generations of the family, ranging from ages 2 to 74, posed around 1927 for this portrait. From left to right are Lillian German Kaffitz, Florence Kaffitz Peterman (who lived to age 101), Martha Anderson German, and Alice Peterman, who later married Henri Lefebvre. (Courtesy Alice Lefebvre.)

Elmer Kaffitz, born to John and Lillian German Kaffitz in 1910, grew up to be a master stonemason, always in demand and able to pick and choose his jobs. The Cherryville cemetery stone wall is a sample of his work. Also a great storyteller, he was once overheard describing a bikini purchased by one of his daughters as "nothing but a bandana and a double-barreled sling shot." (Courtesy Alice Lefebvre.)

Sisters Sara Elizabeth (left) and Jennie Potts strike a fashionable pose with their parasols on a hot summer day in 1908 at the family's homestead on what is now Oak Grove Road. Sara Elizabeth died at age 28 in 1911. Jennie, who was five years younger, lived to age 83. She was married twice, first to Winfield Allen, a stonemason who died early on, and then to William Race. (Courtesy William B. Potts.)

This well-dressed group is believed to be at a church outing of local residents around 1912. From left to right are an unidentified woman holding the hand of an unidentified boy, Blanche D. Conover, Alice Suydam, four unidentified, David T. Conover holding his son Charles, an unidentified man, young Leigh Conover in front, and Wallace Suydam. (Courtesy Virginia and Brevoort C. Conover.)

34

William Marvin Volk posed with his tiny wheelbarrow in 1905. He was born and died in the family's home, the third generation on the Cherryville farm. For his care of the land and work in the community, he is cited on the wall of honor at Holcombe-Jimison Farmstead Museum. He and his wife, the former Edna Stout, had three sons, John, Douglas, and Lawrence. (Courtesy Volk family collection.)

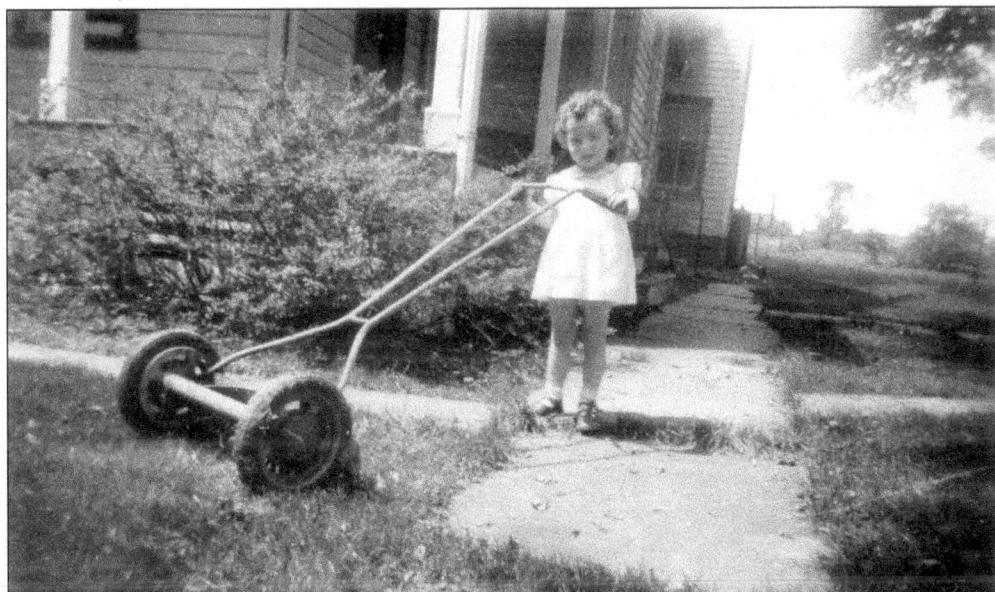

In this photograph from about 1948, Laura Zell Volk is mowing the yard at Maple Glen Farm in Cherryville, her family homestead. The daughter of Lawrence Volk and Zell Warren, she is the fifth generation of her family to live in the house, which is now solar powered. She married Todd Zimmerman of Ho-Ho-Kus. They have two sons, Brian and Christopher. (Courtesy Volk family collection.)

This formal portrait of Minnie Kneiper Miller (left), her daughter Bertha, and her husband, Charles, was taken around 1917. The couple moved from Elizabeth, where Charles worked for the Singer Sewing Machine Company, to a Franklin farm, now a polo field. When Charles and Minnie died in 1942 and 1959, respectively, Bertha's brother George took over the farm. He sold it out of the family in the 1990s. (Courtesy Charles W. Eichlin.)

On February 5, 1925, Jennie Potts posed in a snow cave to emphasize the effect of a storm that, according to Willis W. Vail's diary, began on January 29. It came with strong winds that drove deep drifts across roads and kept them blocked for days. Mail was rerouted and school buses did not run. Some students made their way to the train to get to Flemington High School. (Courtesy William B. Potts.)

In 1925, 19-year-old Raymond Mathews cut quite a figure in his bow tie, knickers, and boater hat at the ready. Everyone agrees on that, but no one will even guess why he was standing where he was for the photograph. He married Myrtle Isabel Hann, and they had two daughters, Marjorie and Joan, and a son, Harold. Raymond was a truck farmer on what is now Locust Grove Road. (Courtesy Joan Mathews.)

Six-foot, 7-inch Russell Little dwarfed his wife, the former Beatrice Smith, as he did everyone in the township. It is said that in his old age, he walked from his house on the south end of Pittstown to the inn on the north end and always checked the parking lot for dropped coins. He often found some, making his morning constitutional not only healthful but also profitable. (Courtesy R. Seymour and family.)

August W. Knispel, who was later Franklin's mayor 11 times in his 33 years on the township committee, stands at left on the Knispel farm in 1932. His grandmother, Pauline Boar Knispel, holds the horse's reins; his sister, Pauline, is at right. The others are unidentified cousins. The milk house, pigpen, and machine shed are seen behind them but were later relocated to other areas. (Courtesy August W. Knispel.)

The Marauda family poses at their farm on Oak Grove Road in the 1930s. From left to right are (first row) Marcel, son of Albert and Madeleine; Paul, Albert's brother; and an unidentified man; (second row) Albert Marauda; his wife, Madeleine; their young daughter Alice; and an unidentified couple. Albert, Paul, and Madeleine all emigrated from Italy and became American citizens. They are buried in Locust Grove Cemetery. (Courtesy Marauda family.)

At the Leusenring farm (now Snowden) on Springhill Road during the 1930s, the field team also helped entertain guests. Alice Leusenring sits astride Fanny (left) with her father, Hugo, holding the reins. Her visiting cousin Edith Miljes is on Prince with Ed Grievison controlling the reins. The horses were mother and son, and Prince always tried to make "mom" do all the work. (Courtesy Aller family.)

A swim in the Capoolong Creek, which appears considerably swelled from rain, was a popular summer pastime. The young boys are William Porter (left), age six, and John Porter, age three. Their mother, Addie Potts Porter (right), and her sister-in-law Leda Potts Porter stand behind them. Their bathing suits and kneesocks were quite the rage in 1925 but seem quaint by today's standards. (Courtesy Janice and Mike Parichuk.)

Farm families were usually large and guests only occasional, so siblings had to learn to entertain each other. A lot of things on a farm were adapted for young folks' play. Tire swings were especially popular. Just look at the smiles on these children's faces on the Marauda farm in the 1930s. The young fellow at bottom left is waiting for his new teeth to grow in. (Courtesy Marauda family.)

The sons of George and Naomi Aller, James (left) and Nathan seem nonchalant about that great worm fence (a fence of crossed rails that create a zigzag pattern) and the beautiful view of their Upper Kingtown Road farm behind them. James, who lived to age 82, was a lifelong farmer. He married Alice Leusenring and had seven children. Nathan became an electrician, married Dorothy Frizzell, had two children, and died at age 59. (Courtesy Aller family.)

The next best thing to hanging tires in trees for swings was rolling them in races. Who can go the fastest, the straightest, and the farthest? Poised to find out are, from left to right, seven-year-old Richard Conley (son of William and Hilda Conley) and nine-year-old Robert Charles Wenzel and 12-year-old James Thomas Wenzel (sons of Hugo and June Wenzel). What else was a young boy to do for fun in 1954? (Courtesy Buch and Wenzel families.)

Galvanized steel wash tubs were indispensable on farms. Everyone had a few for laundry day, butchering day, canning day, bath day, or for just taking a cool soak on a hot summer day. Marie Conover, age seven, and her first cousin Natalie Snyder, age four, prove the point in 1935. The girls' mothers, Anna and Marie Miller, were twin sisters. (Courtesy Virginia and Brevoort C. Conover.)

Buch family members gathered for a photograph in the spring of 1941 at their home on Whitebridge Road where Louis Buch settled in the 1920s after moving from New York City. From left to right are (first row) Gloria Buch, Mary Buch, and Frank Buch; (second row) Raymond Buch, Helen Wenzel (partially hidden), Anna Zajak, June Buch Wenzel, and Jack MacIlroy. (Courtesy Buch and Wenzel families.)

The Nelson and Anna Conover children, Marie and Brevoort, were still thrilled with their Christmas tricycle in the spring of 1938 when they got new hound dogs, which later helped hunt rabbits. Brevoort appears to be ahead of his time in wearing a hard hat but really has on a soft leather helmet with goggles like pilots wore then in open-air cockpits. (Courtesy Virginia and Brevoort C. Conover.)

Augustus E. Snyder, on the ladder, tries to paint the clapboard siding of his newly enlarged house (note the stickers on the window panes) at Still House Farm in Quakertown in 1943. James Griffith, his three-year-old grandson, wants to help. The Snyders bought the farm from Albert Shepperd in 1933. From the age of seven, Griffith summered at the farm until it was sold in 1961 to Dan Bacon. (Courtesy H. James and Katherine E. Griffith.)

George Miller, son of Charles and Minnie, was born on September 27, 1925. To celebrate his sixth birthday, his parents hosted a party on their farm, where today polo is played. The guests are, from left to right, Brevoort C. Conover, William Suydam, Marie Conover, Gene Leaver, George Miller (with his arms folded), Glen Leaver, Margaret and Hazel Lawson, Elizabeth Dissler, and Emma Lawson. (Courtesy Virginia and Brevoort C. Conover.)

LaRee VanWyck and Elsie Wheat shared a Pepsi in 1938, fell in love, married in 1940, and had two daughters, Laureen and Judith. An enterprising young man, VanWyck bought and dismantled the Cherryville Baptist Church horse sheds and took down two houses elsewhere. He used the lumber to build his family's house on three-quarters of an acre of land sold to him by Marvin Volk for $1. (Courtesy LaRee VanWyck.)

Celebrating having just been married, Eleanor Reper and William Reading sit atop his festively decorated 1927 Nash at the end of Leaver Lane in 1946. There was plenty to celebrate since Reading was home safely from World War II, where he served two years in the U.S. Navy's fuel division. The couple was married 57 years until Eleanor died. They had three children, William Jr., Susan, and Thomas. (Courtesy William Reading.)

Dorothy Miller and Robert Sterner pose at the Quakertown United Methodist Church altar following their wedding on October 29, 1960. Miller was born on what is now known as Linden Lane Farm on Quakertown Road and lived there until her father, Adolph, sold it in 1951. Adolph was one of the directors of the Egg Auction in Flemington. (Courtesy Dot and Bob Sterner.)

This Bauer family portrait was taken in 1949. From left to right are (first row) Joyce and Henry (children of Mildred and Henry Bauer) and Doris (daughter of Ann and Martin Bauer); (second row) Ann Bauer Shurr, John Bauer, Francis Eckert Bauer, and Martin Bauer; (third row) Tony Bauer, Marie Bauer, Lee Shurr, Tess Schmidt Bauer, Joe Bauer, Mildred Smithers Bauer, Henry Bauer, Ann Fisher Bauer, William Bauer, and Marlene Bauer. (Courtesy Bauer family.)

Laura Trimmer Potts, shown here with her oldest daughter Edna, was appointed as postmaster for Sidney on April 26, 1906, becoming the first female postmaster in Franklin. In the ensuing 103 years, only six other females have served Franklin. The Sidney Post Office was opened in 1832, discontinued in July 1837, and reopened in September of the same year. It closed permanently in 1909. (Courtesy Janice and Mike Parichuk.)

The tiny Quakertown Post Office was established on April 2, 1828, and was housed in several buildings around the village. It remains a favorite stop for catching up on village news, like Albert Shepperd (left) and postal clerk Thisbe Leaver Conover seem to be doing in 1969. One resident said of the post office, "It has easy parking and if I see someone there, I know them." (Courtesy Kenneth and Margaret Shepperd.)

The daughters of Charles and Dorothy Mathews Smith, seven-year-old Nancy (front) and 18-year-old Catherine, dressed in their Easter finery in 1957 to attend the Quakertown United Methodist Church. Nancy married Ronald Mathews; Catherine became a county sheriff's officer and died in 1999. Their father was a milk deliveryman for Bush Dairies in Flemington. (Courtesy Ron and Nancy Mathews.)

Michael Mergentime drinks spring water on his family farm near Cherryville, which he and his three siblings, Andrea, Stephen, and twin sister Valerie, now own. Michael and Stephen are chairman and president, respectively, of a specialty engineering and construction firm and donated its services to put a new foundation under Franklin's 1837 one-room schoolhouse, saving it for posterity. Both are graduates of the elementary school where the historic building sits. (Photograph by Walter Chandoha.)

Quakertown residents enjoy a summer picnic on July 4, 1950. Clockwise from left to right are Elizabeth Polacsek, Jean Taylor Polacsek, Fred Polacsek, Evangeline Vail Snyder, and Belle Gough Vail. Willis W. Vail, Fred's old scoutmaster and friend, took the photograph and noted in his diary that the afternoon temperature was only 73 degrees and there was a brief shower. (Courtesy Fred and Jean Polacsek.)

The late J. Edward Stout stands at the Peak, a modest promontory some 40 feet above a Capoolong Creek tributary. It was this site that prompted the title of his township history book *Facts and Fantasies of Franklin*. The Peak is so entwined with a 1902 newspaper tale of fantasy—repeated in his book—about sliding rocks, subterranean passageways, and hieroglyphics, that some people doubt its existence. (Courtesy *Hunterdon Democrat*.)

Three

FARMING THE FIELDS

As late as the 1930s, large draft horses like these were still working the fields. Siblings Brevoort C. and Marie Conover are riding on the front horse, while cousin William "Bud" Conover is on the other horse. Grandfather Brevoort W. Conover poses behind the corn cultivator at his Pittstown farm in this photograph from about 1935. (Courtesy Virginia and Brevoort C. Conover.)

A *c.* 1910 wheat harvest at a Pittstown farm shows a three-horse team pulling a grain binder. The binder cut the wheat and tied the stalks into sheaves. The sheaves were then arranged into groups called shocks, seen on the right. These shocks withstood all kinds of weather until they could be taken to the barn and threshed. (Courtesy Virginia and Brevoort C. Conover.)

Albert Shepperd, foreground, and a friend are seen shocking corn at Still House Farm in Quakertown in the 1930s. The cornstalks are being tied and stacked together in the field to dry. This time-honored method had been done for centuries. (Courtesy Kenneth and Margaret Shepperd.)

Descendents of James German (left) know he was born in 1852 and died in 1926, but they do not know when he bought his farm near Cherryville where he stands with his team and disk harrow in the early 1900s. An unidentified helper is ready to start the work. Disk harrows were drawn over plowed fields to break up clods and level the soil for seeding. (Courtesy Alice Lefebvre.)

Adolph Miller (Mueller) immigrated to America about 1900 and lived in Bayonne until purchasing a farm in Cherryville around 1923. This 1924 photograph shows Adolph (left) and his son Christian setting up wheat shocks on their farm, which today is known as Linden Lane Farm. (Courtesy Virginia and Brevoort C. Conover.)

In a photograph dated August 18, 1939, farmer Ludwig Buch of Whitebridge Road has hooked a threshing machine to his Massey Harris four-wheel-drive tractor for power. In earlier days, wooden flails were used for the purpose of beating grain from the husk or stalk. Modern equipment like the one shown here made the task easier and faster. (Courtesy Buch and Wenzel families.)

A giant pea sheller sits at the Frank A. Mathews farm on Locust Grove Road, just outside of Quakertown proper. This c. 1938 photograph includes 30-year-old Raymond Mathews and other family members. The harvest must have been enormous to require such a massive piece of equipment. (Courtesy Ted and Janice Wene Haas.)

This harvest wagon is being hoisted so that every ear of dried corn reaches the conveyor, which then fills the corn crib. It must have been a bumper year for corn since the crib appears full to the brim. Wilson Compton (right) proudly sits on the wagon in 1917 at his farm at the corner of Locust Grove and Pittstown Roads. (Courtesy Mary Bodine and family.)

This 1920s McCormick-Deering iron-wheeled tractor was a big advance over harnessing up the team for farm work at Highland Farm on West Sidney Road, and two unidentified female Tinnes family members seem to approve. The farm was home to Michael and Susanna Farr Tinnes and their 12 children, born between 1910 and 1933. (Courtesy Tinnes family.)

Native Americans grew maize (corn), and early Franklin settlers have continued the practice to present day. Leaver Stout, on the tractor, and young Charles Mathews are seen here planting corn on Mother's Day around 1940. The Stout farm was on Locust Grove Road in Quakertown. Mathews still runs his own farm in the village today. (Courtesy Marjorie and Charles Mathews.)

"Cow" corn is being harvested at the Mathews farm on Locust Grove Road about 1960 by Harold F. Mathews, who inherited the farm from his father, Frank A. Mathews. Today most corn grown in the township is for animal feed, but residents eagerly await summer's first ears of sweet corn at local farm stands. (Courtesy Ron and Nancy Mathews.)

Corn harvest in November 1945 appeared to be a fun time for three-year-old Charles W. Eichlin. His parents, Jesse and Bertha Miller Eichlin, ran a farm at the corner of Croton and Franklin School Roads south of Quakertown. In prior years, farmers took their corn to gristmills to be ground for use in corn bread, corn pudding, and even in animal feed. (Courtesy Charles W. Eichlin.)

Frances Peters Passerello stands with an amazing 14-foot-tall cornstalk at the Passerello farm in Cherryville in 1947. A lifelong resident of Franklin, she married Nunzio Passerello, and along with their children, James T. and Judith, ran a large farm for many years. (Courtesy James and Mary Passerello and Judith Winfield.)

It is common knowledge that goats are mischievous creatures. This agile pet at the Schultz farm along Whitebridge Road occupied itself by going up and down a ladder to the barn loft and was caught in the act in this 1940s photograph. (Courtesy Schultz family.)

Growing up on a farm in the country is always an adventure for children. Ten-year-old Kenneth Shepperd (left) and Allen Trout hold pet bunnies in front of wheat shocks in this 1932 photograph. Still House Farm, where Shepperd lived, is in Quakertown. (Courtesy Kenneth and Margaret Shepperd.)

Brevoort C. Conover was born on September 13, 1930, in Pittstown, the son of Nelson Shepherd Conover and Anna Natalie Miller. In 1948, one of his 4-H projects included raising 200 pheasant chicks to 15 weeks and releasing them. He went on to attend Rutgers University's College of Agriculture and later became a 4-H agent for Warren County. (Courtesy Virginia and Brevoort C. Conover.)

William Tinnes gives his pet goat a squeeze around 1931. Tinnes was born in 1924 at Tinnes Corner (formerly Highland Farm) and still lives there with his wife of 55 years, Elizabeth. He farmed all his life and still lends a hand to younger farmers in Franklin Township. (Courtesy Tinnes family.)

Judith Passerello picks apples on her family's Cherryville farm in the late 1950s. Apples have been a staple Franklin commodity since Colonial days. They were pressed into cider, sliced into pies, mashed into sauces, and dried for winter storage. Stills were located on some farms to convert apple juice into "Jersey Lightning." (Courtesy James and Mary Passerello and Judith Winfield.)

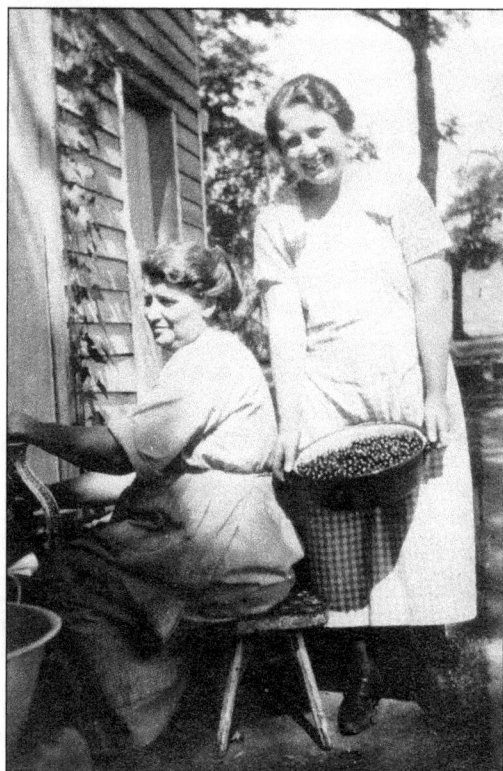

Wilhelmina Miller (left) and her friend Mrs. Kelinski pit cherries at the Miller farm in Cherryville around 1924. Cherryville is said to have been named in 1839 in honor of the Cherry family, who possibly owned land there, but extensive research has not revealed the truth of that. It is more likely that the village was named Cherryville for its abundance of cherry orchards. (Courtesy Virginia and Brevoort C. Conover.)

In 1879, the *Hunterdon Democrat* reported, "Franklin Township is the peach-yielding township of the County." Farmers delivered their harvest to the Pittstown Railroad station for distribution to distant points. Wagons loaded with baskets overflowing with ripe peaches are shown pulling into the station in 1897. (Courtesy Enrico and Chiara Chandoha.)

After the Civil War, the New Jersey peach industry was hurt by southern fruit shipped north by rail weeks before local produce ripened. The industry's second blow was the San Jose scale (blight). Today, as seen in the 1940s at Still House Farm in Quakertown, smaller orchards dot Franklin's landscape and farm stands are filled with luscious peaches. (Courtesy H. James and Katherine E. Griffith.)

Brevoort W. Conover was influential statewide in agricultural circles because he saw the need to improve the purchasing power of farmers and the marketing of their products. He helped establish the Dairyman's League Cooperative Association, a milk marketing group, and held a picnic for them at his farm in 1929. Years later, he was named to the wall of honor at the Holcomb-Jimison Farmstead Museum. (Courtesy Virginia and Brevoort C. Conover.)

As the saying goes, "party till the cows come home." When these contented bovines at the Passerello farm come home to the barn across from the old Colonial dwelling, they use the sidewalk that starts a quarter-mile from the main road. This humorous scene was photographed in the 1940s. (Courtesy James and Mary Passerello and Judith Winfield.)

Jennie Potts, daughter of William B. Potts, is seen around 1908 with her pet cow Rose. The Potts family lived in Oak Grove on a farm passed down for four generations. Cows have always been an integral part of farm life. They supplied milk, which was used to make butter, cheese, and, the all-time favorite of rural farm children, ice cream. (Courtesy William B. Potts.)

The 100-acre Conover farm spanned two sides of the Pittstown-Quakertown Road. Cows had to be herded from the pasture on one side to the barn on the other for the evening milking. Marie Conover (right) and her husband, Emmett Russell, were seen handling that end-of-the-day chore for her parents, Nelson and Anna Conover, around 1947. (Courtesy Virginia and Brevoort C. Conover.)

Harvesting hay at the Knispel farm on West Sidney Road in 1939 was heavy work. The hay was cut with a horse-drawn sickle bar, allowed to dry, and gathered into heaps by hand. Here August Knispel uses a long handled three-tined fork to pitch heaps of dry hay onto the wagon; his son August W. helped spread it. Tillie Burkoff, a family friend, is along for the ride. (Courtesy August W. Knispel.)

From left to right, George Aller and sons James and Nathan are tossing field grass with a horse-drawn hay rake in 1931 at their farm on Upper Kingtown Road. Hot, dry days were necessary for a good harvest. Hay was, and still is, a valuable commodity in Franklin. It is used to feed cows, horses, sheep, alpacas, and goats over the winter. (Courtesy Aller family.)

From left to right, siblings Harrie, Florence, and Hugo Wenzel pose with Mr. Lake in 1932 around a wheelbarrow full of corn stalks at Glenside Farm on Sidney School Road. Behind them towers a giant heap of hay waiting to be stored in the mow of the barn. (Courtesy Buch and Wenzel families.)

Local farmers used "real" horsepower through the end of World War II, and then mechanical balers that created the rectangular bales so familiar to everyone became the norm. Esther Grasekamp Peterson, matriarch of the Peterson farm in Cherryville, drives a 1951 Ford tractor full of baled hay in this 1962 photograph. Helpers are Ted Bauer (left) and John Kuhl. (Courtesy Peterson family.)

On Malt Day, farmers from Franklin and nearby townships took wagonloads of grains to the Pittstown train depot to be shipped to areas such as Newark. Barley, rye, and hops were necessary ingredients for making beer and other alcoholic beverages. Prohibition, enacted in 1919, must have brought a stop to this two-decade-long practice. (Courtesy Franklin Archives.)

Early settlers relied on water to power a large, up-and-down gash saw for cutting wood. They were replaced by water-powered circular saws in the mid-1800s. In the 1930s, from left to right, Russ Wolverton, Walter Eichlin, and Samuel Willson used a gas-powered engine to run a large circular blade to cut wood on what is now Marve Farm on Whitebridge Road. (Courtesy Charles W. Eichlin.)

The barn at right on West Sidney Road, built on the foundation of an earlier barn that burned around 1951, burned again in 1964. The Tinnes family added the middle structure for their dairy herd, and the second fire ended the dairy business at Highland Farm, but farming continued with other crops. William and Elizabeth Tinnes still own the property, now referred to as Tinnes Corner. (Courtesy Tinnes family.)

This farm on West Sidney Road looks a little different today than when it was purchased by Romanian immigrants John and Pauline Farr Tinnes in the 1920s. They had dairy cows, grew tomatoes, and owned three school buses, which both John and Pauline drove. Pauline was loved for treating her riders to ice cream cones on the last day of school. John was mayor in 1955. (Courtesy Jane R. Smith.)

Because hogs are readily propagated in large numbers and are relatively inexpensive to keep, they are profitable animals to raise. Here David T. Conover tends his hogs in the 1920s. Conover, born in 1875, was raised on the family farm in Cherryville but later lived in Pittstown. He was a farmer and a livestock dealer. (Courtesy Virginia and Brevoort C. Conover.)

Contrary to popular prejudices, pigs are not filthy animals. When allowed to run free in pastures or kept in pens, they will be observed to maintain a high degree of cleanliness, and as pets, they are often trainable like dogs. In 1936, Mary Compton (right) and her city cousin Mildred are playfully pulling a pig's tail on the family's Locust Grove Road farm. (Courtesy Mary Bodine and family.)

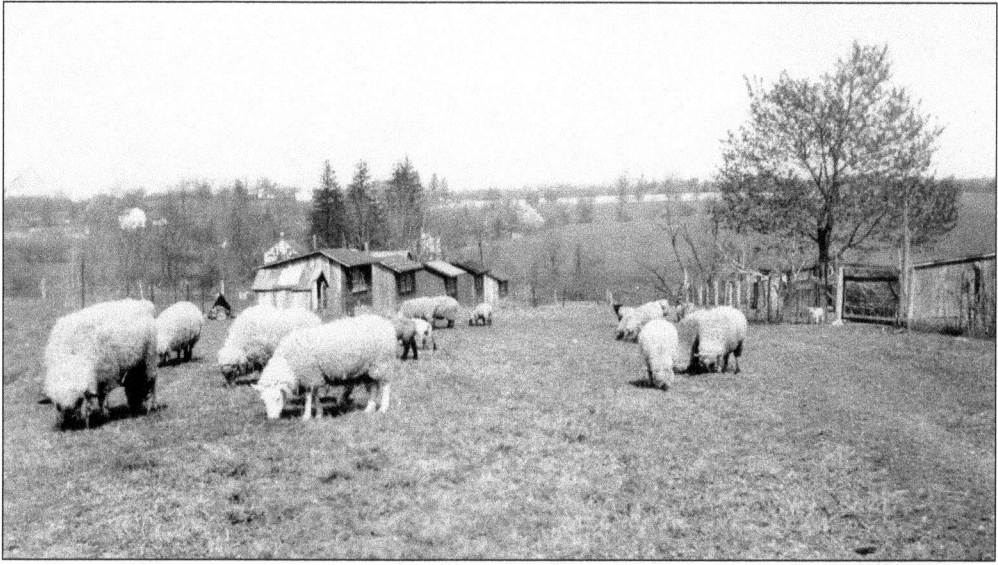

Sheep graze on the pastoral hills of the Knispel farm in this 1948 photograph. August W. Knispel raised these Hampshire sheep and says that they were good wool producers. He had 30 head and sheared them himself, then he bundled each fleece with paper twine. Rutgers Agricultural Extension Service provided a wool pool market for local farmers. (Courtesy August W. Knispel.)

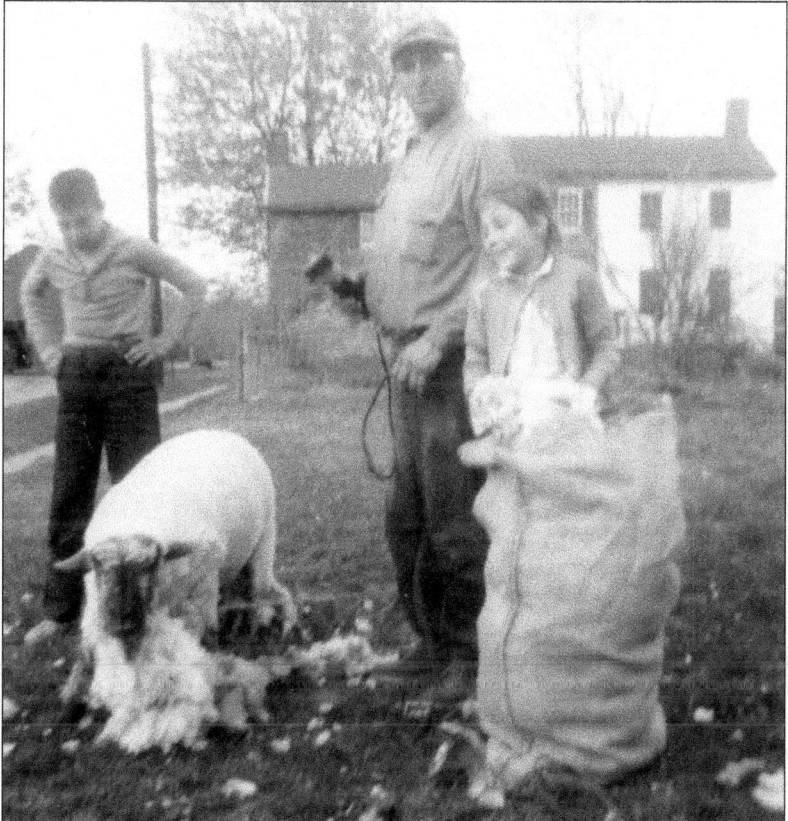

In Colonial days, sheep were raised primarily for wool. By the early 1800s, different breeds were introduced from Europe to improve American strains. Raising sheep declined by 1900 but picked up again after World War II. James (left) and Judith Passerello and their father, Nunzio, attest that shearing sheep was a family affair in 1962. (Courtesy James and Mary Passerello and Judith Winfield.)

Tomatoes, members of the nightshade family, were once thought to be poisonous, but after the mid-1800s, attitudes changed towards this delectable fruit. Fields in Franklin were full of these juicy, red orbs by the late 1800s. Nunzio Passerello of Cherryville packs overflowing baskets of tomatoes into the back of his pickup truck in the 1940s. (Courtesy James and Mary Passerello and Judith Winfield.)

Susanna Farr Tinnes (right) oversees her sons as they pack their great tomato harvest into baskets for shipping in the early 1940s. Starting in the late 1800s, market tomatoes were transported to New York by rail. Canneries sprung up throughout the county from Lambertville to Bloomsbury, and before World War II, local farmers were contracting to sell their crops to the Campbell Soup Company. (Courtesy Tinnes family.)

The Freehold Produce Company opened a plant in Quakertown in the 1930s and moved the operation to Cherryville in 1937. Local farm women helped pack field-grown tomatoes for shipping to supermarkets. In October 1937, from left to right, Helen Smith, Thisbe Leaver Conover, and Bertha Miller Eichlin are seen taking a break outside the packing plant. (Courtesy Charles W. Eichlin.)

While Nunzio Passerello was busy growing tomatoes, his wife, Frances (pictured), was cultivating her field of dahlias in the 1940s. Once a week they took eggs, vegetables, and flowers to Elizabeth, where they sold the produce out of their truck. (Courtesy James and Mary Passerello and Judith Winfield.)

Before the 1900s, Franklin farmers raised poultry and eggs for the local market. The incubator changed everything, and hatcheries annually produced millions of chickens in Hunterdon County. Franklin had its share of this volume, as the following photographs show. Around 1905, young Charles Carroll Wright is feeding his chickens on the family farm on Pittstown Road near Locust Grove Road. (Courtesy Mary Bodine and family.)

Charles W. Eichlin, pictured at age two in 1942, helps his grandfather Walter throw feed to the chickens on the Eichlin farm at the corner of Croton and Franklin School Roads. By this date, most Franklin farms had numerous chicken houses on their property and supplemented their income by selling chickens and eggs. (Courtesy Charles W. Eichlin.)

The Knispel family started farming on Oak Grove Road in Croton, where Caroline Knispel is seen feeding geese in 1927. She made pillows and feather-bed mattresses from their chest feathers. The barn at right was built by her husband, August Knispel, about 1925. The family moved to a farm on West Sidney Road in 1928. The Knispel's son August W. continued to farm there until 2006. (Courtesy August W. Knispel.)

The February 14, 1947, *Hunterdon Democrat* reported that a New Hampshire red pullet on the Passerello farm, scornful of a 6-ounce egg laid by a leghorn in Pittstown, "got down to business and laid one of the most spacious eggs ever deposited in the County Agent's office." It weighed 7 ounces and was 7 7/8 inches long. Theodore Peters is shown with the all-star chickens. (Courtesy James and Mary Passerello and Judith Winfield.)

In the 1950s, Clifford E. and Melda Chambre Snyder had a large chicken operation at their Locust Grove Road farm. Clifford, the third generation to own the farm, increased its size to 450 acres by 1964. At his death, most of the land was conveyed to Rutgers University by his widow for an experimental station. Rutgers continues Franklin's tomato heritage and every August hosts the Great Tomato Tasting, attracting hundreds. (Courtesy Franklin Archives.)

Madeleine Marauda, seen feeding chickens in the late 1930s, is standing in front of a long, low building called a laying house at the family farm in Oak Grove. Notice the farm cat at lower right. Homegrown felines knew not to mess with the chickens and got along with virtually all the farm animals while policing the barns for rodents. (Courtesy Marauda family.)

Two farm hands, Russel Botsford (left) and Carol Heisler, are candling and sorting eggs at the Adolph Miller farm in Quakertown in the 1960s. Most of the eggs ended up at the Flemington Cooperative Egg Auction Market, which was organized in 1930 to help local farmers sell to larger outside markets. (Courtesy Dot and Bob Sterner.)

Natalie Lange Schultz, her grandson Chester August Schultz Jr., and her husband, August, are seen at the family farm on Whitebridge Road in 1952 after collecting wire baskets full of eggs laid by their chickens that day. The eggs then had to be cleaned and packed in crates for hauling by truck to the Flemington Cooperative Egg Auction Market. Chickens too old to lay were sold for food. (Courtesy Schultz family.)

The Conover farm on the Pittstown-Quakertown Road, purchased in 1897, was sold out of the family in 1951. This photograph shows the equipment auction held that year. By 1955, a later owner created Franklin's first development, known as Quaker Hill, by selling the land across the road from the house in approximately 3-acre building lots. (Courtesy Virginia and Brevoort C. Conover.)

Johnson German (1894–1985) of Cherryville (right) teaches Samuel Chandoha how to sharpen a scythe in the late 1960s. German never took to modern things like electricity and automobiles. He worked odd jobs on Franklin farms in exchange for breakfast or lunch. Dressed in his best attire, he attended every day of the Flemington Fair each year. (Photograph by Walter Chandoha.)

Four

GETTING AROUND TOWN

A dandy gentleman poses in his two-horse open sleigh in front of the Joseph B. Probasco house in Quakertown on a snowy winter day around 1890. Sleighs were the best mode of transportation on slippery Franklin roads. The Friends, who built their meetinghouse on the opposite corner, owned the property in the background until 1861, when it sold to cabinetmaker William Probasco for his son Joseph. (Courtesy Jerry and Karen Kuiper.)

Linden Mathews (left) is being chauffeured south on Croton Road away from the center of Quakertown by an unidentified friend around 1917, prior to going to Europe to fight in the trenches of World War I. The American flag on the fender shows the patriotic spirit of the community at the time. The dwelling in the background at center was owned then by George and Nancy Race. (Courtesy Marjorie and Charles Mathews.)

Drive Looking West, Cherryville, N. J.   Pub. by A. S. Everitt.

This is what the view looked like going west from Cherryville to Quakertown in the late 1800s. Although the endless expanse of farmland and worm fences looked pastoral, the road surface was muddy, uneven, riddled with holes, and full of wagon-wheel ruts. Local travelers, animals, and carriages returned from their sojourns caked in mud or dust, depending on the season. (Courtesy Ella M. Haver.)

Burris Snyder, age 57, and Evangeline Vail, age 44, are setting off from the Snyder farm on Locust Grove Road with a fur throw over their laps on this chilly November 19, 1913, morning. After posing for this photograph taken by Evangeline's brother Willis W. Vail, the couple continued to High Bridge to be married. The rest of the wedding party went by automobile. (Courtesy Hunterdon County Historical Society.)

One of the early motorized vehicles on Franklin's roads around 1913 was this touring car with wooden-spoke wheels, gaslight lanterns, a retractable roof, and tufted seats like those on fancy horse-drawn carriages. S. R. Reed was at the wheel, with Peter Conover at his side. In back are, from left to right, Jean Reed (hidden), Ruth Gould, and Lloyd Conover. A broken down horse-drawn bakery wagon is off the road at right. (Courtesy Virginia and Brevoort C. Conover.)

Merchants, farmers, and other citizens of Franklin welcomed the advent of railroads in the late 1800s. It made for quick and easy transport of people, goods, and livestock. The Pittstown station opened in 1891 and is depicted in this c. 1900 postcard. Although the station closed in 1968 and service ended, the depot still stands awaiting restoration. The track bed is now a hiking trail. (Courtesy Franklin Archives.)

In this 1922 photograph, Chester A. Schultz is all dressed up to go on a long journey to New York City from Grandin station. The first passenger trains came through this station in 1875. Schultz and his family were in Franklin Township visiting relatives on Whitebridge Road and eventually moved out to their own farm here in 1931. (Courtesy Schultz family.)

Tooling around the Compton farm on Locust Grove Road are Wilson Compton and his daughters Mary (left) and Fannie "at the wheel," around 1926. This early farm vehicle was converted into a flatbed truck for hauling grain, hay, and other heavy materials. The Compton home, family car, barn, wagon house, and two-story chicken house can be seen in the background. (Courtesy Mary Bodine and family.)

When a major ice storm hit Franklin Township on January 1, 1948, Nelson S. Conover carefully drove around Pittstown and Quakertown the next day to photograph the damage. Here power lines are down on the Pittstown-Quakertown Road. According to Willis W. Vail, the power went out around 8:00 p.m. on January 1 and did not come back on until January 7. (Courtesy Virginia and Brevoort C. Conover.)

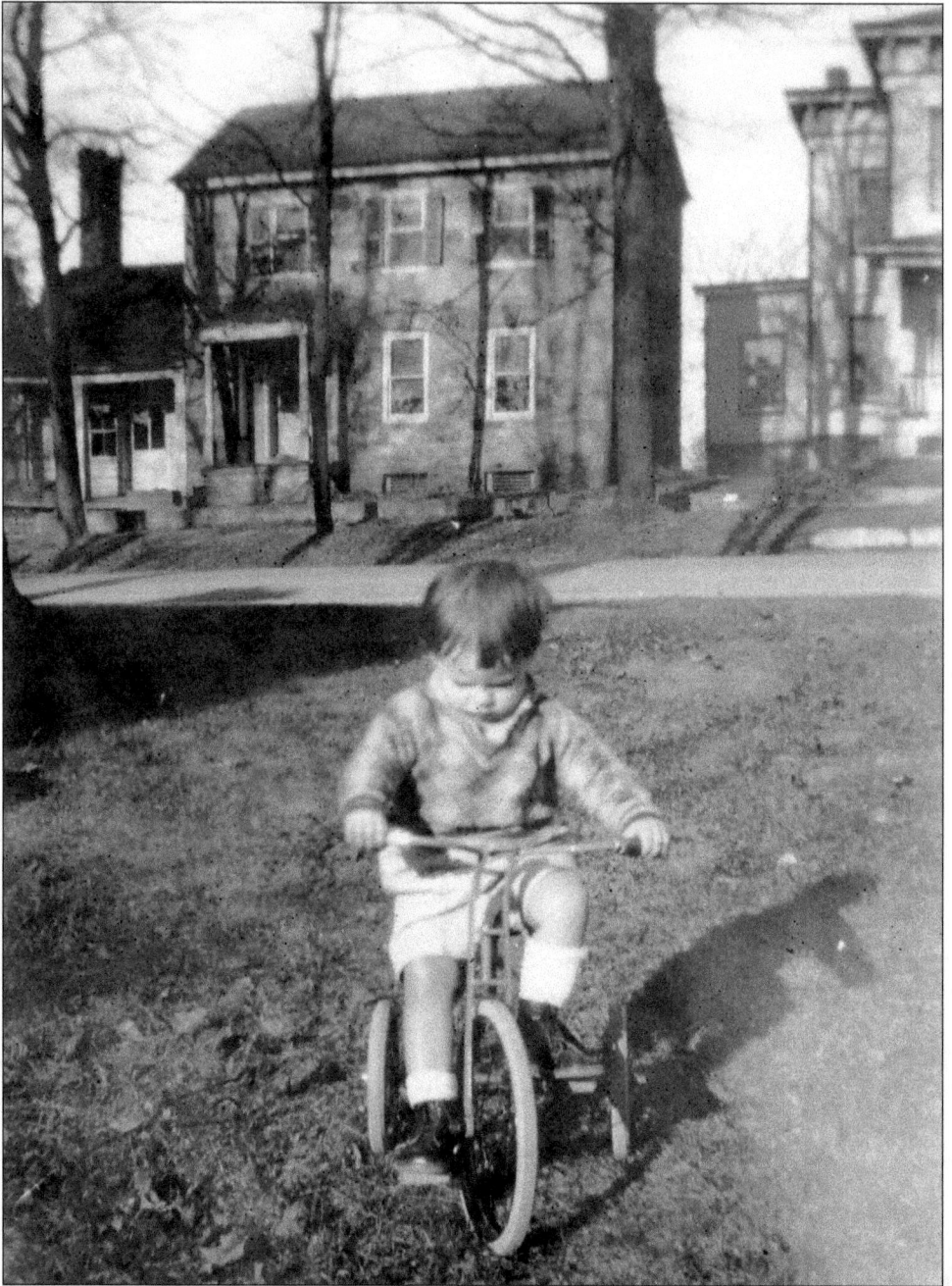

This 1932 photograph shows that three-year-old Charles Mathews knew the best way to get around Quakertown, and it did not require any gasoline, hay, or expensive upkeep. He still resides on a farm down a lane in the village with his wife, Marjorie, and poodle Peaches and runs a farm stand with seasonal produce. He has been known to put in 2,000 tomato plants to serve his customers. Behind him is the stone William Probasco dwelling, built of local squared stones. The large, two-story addition in the Federal style was built around 1814 onto a much earlier wing. At right is a portion of the c. 1867 John Harned Vail clapboard house in the Italianate style. (Courtesy Marjorie and Charles Mathews.)

Horses were a staple on Franklin farms for both work and play. Here Bob the horse pulls Alice Marauda (right) and an unidentified girl in a cart on the family farm in Oak Grove around 1930. To the left of Bob are free-range chickens and a large fenced-in family garden. The farmhouse is partially visible behind the children. (Courtesy Marauda family.)

Two young girls pose on large draft horses at the Volk farm in Cherryville in this 1920s photograph. Notice the fly strings that the horses are wearing. As the animal moves, the strings wave and thus keep flies away. This was a practical down-on-the-farm method prior to the invention of modern insecticides. (Courtesy Volk family collection.)

Not old enough to drive the late-1930s coupe parked behind him, Charles W. Eichlin, age three-and a-half, pedals around the family farm at the corner of Croton and Franklin School Roads in 1946. His tricycle, with a hooked-up wagon, shows that he was eager to help his parents, Jesse and Bertha, with any farm chores. (Courtesy Charles W. Eichlin.)

Sarah H. Shepherd Conover plays in the snow with granddaughters Mary (left) and Jean, children of Lloyd and Margaret Conover, at the family farm around 1930. If Sarah was anticipating a great ride, it is obvious from the girls' expressions that she was not going to travel very far. After all, they were only "horsing around." (Courtesy Virginia and Brevoort C. Conover.)

In 1913, Ella M. Haver was born near Sidney in the Judge Samuel Johnson house, then owned by her grandfather. She poses in her 1939 four-door Plymouth sedan, which she bought new in Clinton for $650 with money borrowed from her father. In 2009, at age 96, she does good deeds for Franklin citizens, and only recently stopped driving the township's picturesque roads. (Courtesy Ella M. Haver.)

The Chicken Coop Tavern in Sidney was big on promotions to attract customers, like this old-fashioned stagecoach in the 1940s. Bill Williams is at the reins, with "Pop" Bauer riding shotgun. From left to right are (in the coach) Margaret Powell, an unidentified woman, and Mrs. Porter; (standing) Marie Bauer, an unidentified woman, Marge Orban, "Tippy" Fleming, John Powell, Ann Bauer Schuer, and Rowena Winslow Kerr. (Courtesy Bauer family.)

Quakertown and Cherryville are on a high plateau that frequently receives strong winds and severe storms. The blizzard of 1966 on January 22–23 was reported to have hit Hunterdon County the worst. The 22-hour storm dropped 25 inches of snow, but 63-mile-per-hour winds helped create 10- to 15-foot drifts, and the temperature fell below freezing. (Courtesy William Reading.)

A few days after the blizzard of 1966, William Reading drove his 1962 Volkswagen around and about the roads of Franklin to record the event. He parked at the recently plowed crossroads in Cherryville, where lucky residents could get out on the road. Older residents remember that many Franklin roads were not plowed for up to 10 days. (Courtesy William Reading.)

After a severe snowstorm, probably the one in February or March 1947, Chester A. Schultz and some of his neighbors emerged from their warm and cozy homes to shovel out driveways. Since it was a year before the township purchased the Oshkosh snowplowing truck, residents began the awesome task of shoveling Whitebridge Road towards Quakertown, in hopes of reaching the village some day. (Courtesy Schultz family.)

Reenacting an old-time activity, Eugene and Marjorie Schuyler Van Ness are breezing through the bucolic hills of Franklin in a one-horse open sleigh on a sunny winter day in the 1960s. Marjorie was a founder of the American Saddlebred Horse Association of New Jersey, and in 1971, she was the first woman appointed to the New Jersey Board of Agriculture. She also was a trustee of Hunterdon Medical Center. (Photograph by Walter Chandoha.)

Small airplanes were another mode of transportation for local residents and were mostly used for recreation. They kept their aircraft at an airport in the next township but frequently landed and took off from their own properties. In 1948, Preston Hoagland tried to land on the Snyder farm along Locust Grove Road but came in too fast and damaged the front end of the airplane. (Courtesy Ted and Janice Wene Haas.)

Nunzio Passerello won this Farmall tractor pedal car as a door prize at a political function. When his son James became proficient at driving it, he delighted in chauffeuring his little sister Judith around their Cherryville farm in the mid-1950s. Although the tires are now worn down, James still owns this cherished family heirloom. (Courtesy James and Mary Passerello and Judith Winfield.)

Five

EDUCATING THE MIND AND SOUL

Since the mid-1700s, several schools have existed at different times in Franklin. In 1850, a two story, stucco-covered stone academy was erected in Quakertown by subscription. Elias Dalrymple was the third and best-remembered headmaster. Dalrymple was a blacksmith, surveyor, and Civil War veteran. This late-1800s view shows him surrounded by students and adults at the academy property. (Courtesy Mary Bodine and family.)

In the 1990s, Mark Mortensen, owner of a historic home in Quakertown, was removing rotted clapboards on the exterior when he discovered a piece of glass covered in bat guano within the wall. Thinking it was an old window pane that had fallen from the attic, Mortensen took it to the trash. Before tossing it away, he noticed an image on the glass and quickly washed the dirt off with a hose. A print of this glass-plate negative revealed an amazing treasure: it was a photograph of the academy that had once stood on land near the Mortensen home. The picture was probably taken in the late 1800s by teacher Elias Dalrymple, since he was also an accomplished photographer. Dalrymple mentored Willis W. Vail, whose early glass-plate photography graces this book. Notice that the children have moved during the long exposure, creating ghostly images of themselves. (Courtesy Mark and Irene Mortensen.)

A stone schoolhouse stood on this spot on Sidney School Road from 1816 until about 1865. Then a 20-foot-by-30-foot frame building was erected to serve the local children. This was one of the five one-room schoolhouses in Franklin prior to the opening of a consolidated school in 1937 and the only one that no longer exists. The four others are now private residences. (Courtesy Franklin Archives.)

Like Sidney, Cherryville's first school was a stone building. In 1860, a 22-foot-by-30-foot frame structure replaced it. This is the 1927 class, with teacher Miss Robinson (back row, left). The little boy at center in the second row is Fred Polascek. He was living with his grandparents in Cherryville at the time. Today the school is a private residence. (Courtesy Fred and Jean Polascek.)

In 1901, the township committee proposed to purchase land on which to build a schoolhouse in Pittstown. The school was built several years later. This 1929 photograph shows the entire one-room school class, along with their teacher in the back row. This building was sold after the Franklin Township consolidated school opened in 1937. (Courtesy R. Seymour and family.)

A new wood schoolhouse was built in Quakertown in 1912, and shortly afterwards, the stucco-covered stone academy was torn down. Pictured is the 1922 class taught by Mrs. Harrison. Some family names of the children attending were Eichlin, Shepperd, Suydam, Prall, Stout, Allen, Nixon, Toth, Dissler, Haver, Conover, Smith, Oaks, Emery, York, Ryberg, Farr, Ort, and Search. (Courtesy Mary Bodine and family.)

Fittstown N.J.   Grade 2   June 1937
Merry Christmas to you. Brevort
Sincerely Anna B Barber

This is the last second-grade class to attend the Pittstown one-room schoolhouse in June 1937. From left to right are (first row) Ida Mae Piell, Clela Bloom, and Brevoort C. Conover; (second row) Marjorie Barrick, teacher Anna Barber, and Doris Compton. The teacher made Christmas cards from the photograph and sent them to all of her students. (Courtesy Virginia and Brevoort C. Conover.)

Willis W. Vail took this photograph on June 25, 1938, as the old Quakertown one-room schoolhouse was headed for its new destination. His diary entry reads, "Spent the day watching the moving of the schoolhouse up to Wallace Suydam's just south of Sam Trout's, taking all day . . . I took several pictures of it on the way." This building is still a private residence today. (Courtesy Dot and Bob Sterner.)

The new consolidated Franklin Township School opened on September 7, 1937, with about 200 students. Willis W. Vail noted that two loads of crushed stone were laid as temporary walkways. He was the school board treasurer and cared for the school so much that he obtained films and ran the movie projector, gave out candy and oranges at Christmas, and presented all the graduates with calendars. (Courtesy Mary Bodine and family.)

Transportation logistics were interesting in a rural community. Preston Hoagland, pictured here, picked up students in Pittstown and dropped them off at the newly opened school. He then proceeded to Cherryville to pick up students there. Meanwhile, another bus collected children from Sidney and other areas. The opening of Franklin Township School signaled the end of an era. (Courtesy Mary Bodine and family.)

Activities that could never have been imagined in a one-room schoolhouse were now a reality. Here students are working on the Franklin Township School newspaper, the *Flash*, using typewriters and electric mimeograph machines. Clockwise from left to right are John Ezra Wene, Irene Sabo, Edith Hendershot, Edward Swider, Edward Galuska, Eleanor Samantchy, Werna Mathews, and Jeannette Quick. (Courtesy Ted and Janice Wene Haas.)

Franklin Township School's first graduates in 1938 are pictured here. From left to right are (first row) Edward Swider, Marie Bauer, Elmer Dalrymple, Mary Tufo, John McCrea, Mary Compton, Franklin Rozzo, Theresa Tufo, and Edward Kophazy; (second row) Margaret Orban, Peter Nosal, Marion Barrick, John Porter, Rosalie Crampel, Albert Barrick, Laura Schanze, and John McPherson; (third row) Frank Kanak, John Rozbarski, Dankert Arnesen, teacher/principal Sidney Keller, Ina Trout, John Putcher, Alice Peterman, Edward Tinnes, and Mildred Luchinski. (Courtesy Dot and Bob Sterner.)

The 1944 eighth-grade graduates are pictured here. From left to right are (first row) Robert Reper, Floyd Prall, Rose Tinnes, Virginia Rinehart, Irene Podayko, Marjorie Mathews, and Ida Mae Piell; (second row) Earle Lawson, Irene Hommer, Betty Preckwinkle, Mary Buch, Dolores Thompson, and teacher/principal Edith Higgens; (third row) Brevoort C. Conover, Fred Tinnes, Rudy Krebs, and Charles Mathews. (Courtesy Marjorie and Charles Mathews.)

Mrs. Apgar, a substitute teacher, poses with the consolidated school's first and second graders in 1950. Charles W. Eichlin is in the third row, third from the left. Several boys wear Western-style shirts, reflecting the movies and television series that have reached rural Franklin Township by this date. (Courtesy Charles W. Eichlin.)

Being a kindergarten teacher had always been Elsie VanWyck's dream, so when the position was offered at Franklin's kindergarten through eighth-grade school, she gladly signed on and stayed for almost 20 years. She insisted on discipline and manners in her classes and got them, along with the admiration of both the students and their parents. She is shown here in April 1957 with her engaging pupils. (Courtesy LaRee VanWyck.)

Although the name of this school play is long forgotten, the characters include Native Americans, woodland creatures, birds of the forest, children sleeping around a campfire, and Elizabeth Braidwood (center) starring as "the owl." The thespian tradition continues today, as Franklin Theatre Works trains local youth in the performing arts. (Courtesy Braidwood family.)

The first Friends meetinghouse in Quakertown was a log structure with an adjacent burying ground. A stone building replaced it in the mid-1700s, and in 1862, its stones were reused for this structure set farther back from the road. The meetinghouse closed around 1900. In 1923, Willis W. Vail, as caretaker and trustee, opened it once a year for worship. By 1952, the meeting was reestablished and is active today. (Courtesy Hunterdon County Historical Society.)

This 1888 First Day (or Sunday) school at the Friends meetinghouse was open to all community members regardless of their religious affiliation. Names on back of the photograph list numerous members of the Fleming family, along with Waltons, Mathews, Potts, Suydams, and Snyders. The meetinghouse behind may look boarded up but actually the doors and shutters are just closed for an unknown reason. (Courtesy Joan Mathews.)

The Quakertown United Methodist Church was built in 1840 on land donated by George W. Waterhouse. A beautiful, new building in the Queen Anne style replaced the earlier structure in 1879. Situated on a high plateau in the village, as the tallest edifice, the church can be seen for miles around. This makes it prone to lightning strikes, and a major disaster did strike at noon on Sunday, August 4, 1895. Vail noted in his diary, "a portion of the charge left the steeple . . . traveled down an iron truss-rod . . . and finally to the ground . . . Quite a number of people were injured . . . Minnie Frace of Clinton had both shoes torn off . . . seems to be almost the worst case. Kuhl Hoffman's wife quite badly burned . . . Aunt Amy Willson had heel of one shoe torn off, dress and underclothes torn out." Vail reported that most of the congregation suffered injuries or shock. Reporters came from New York and Philadelphia, and over 140 curiosity seekers arrived to view the damage the next day. Minnie Frace died several days later. (Courtesy George and Sandra Baker.)

The Ladies Aid Society at the Quakertown United Methodist Church was known for community service. Posing in front of the Eichlin residence in the 1930s are, from left to right, Lois Mathews, Marjorie (Peg) Eichlin, Mildred Dissler, Helen Burd, Alice McCloughn, Thisbe Leaver Conover, Almeda Crane, Lucy Mathews, unidentified, Hazel Cleaves, Marie Snyder, and Anna Conover. The child in front is Lois Mathews's daughter Mildred. (Courtesy Virginia and Brevoort C. Conover.)

The Quakertown United Methodist Church's children's choir performed on various occasions, such as Children's Day and Christmas. This 1956 photograph shows Charles and Dorothy Mathews Smith's daughter Nancy fourth from the left in the first row. The stained-glass windows behind the choir were installed in 1926. The congregation is still active today, and among its many activities, it sponsors a food pantry in the township. (Courtesy Ron and Nancy Mathews.)

The Cherryville Baptist Church and parsonage are shown alongside rutted dirt roads in this c. 1910 postcard. In 1849, Rev. Edwin R. Hera was the Baptist minister preaching in the Cherryville vicinity. The church was built in 1850 with 49 members, and the adjoining cemetery opened that year with three interments. The parsonage was purchased in 1869, when there were 160 members. This is an active congregation today. (Courtesy Alice Lefebvre.)

The Cherryville Baptist Church Sunday school poses on the church steps in the spring of 1947. From left to right are (first row) Jane Aten, Nancy Preckwinkle, Dorey Preckwinkle, Peggy Ewing, Priscilla Caka, Marilyn Bennett, Judy Aller, Wilber Force, and Helen Hayes; (second row) Chester Weber, Joan Bennett, Anna Claire, Barbara Caka, Myra Zackman, Ruth Ann Hayes, Janet Hayes, and teacher Edna Peterman. (Courtesy Aller family.)

In 1764, the Friends opened a second graveyard on nearby Croton Road for non-Quakers. Known as Nixon Cemetery today, by 1962, it had become overgrown with trees and brush. Russell Little, his young nephew Robert Seymour, and other concerned citizens mapped and gridded the graveyard. Stones were removed, trees and stumps were cleared, and then the gravestones were put back in place. This awesome task took six years. (Courtesy R. Seymour and family.)

The Locust Grove Cemetery was incorporated in 1867 and is located at the west end of Quakertown. This restful and scenic spot holds the remains of many prominent Franklin residents. A stately, arched entrance and fence once existed, as seen in this early 1900s photograph, and must have been removed by the 1930s. (Courtesy Fred and Jean Polascek.)

Six

COMMUNITY SPIRIT

Students from the Quakertown one-room schoolhouse are costumed around 1926 to dance at the annual May Day festival held at the Flemington Fairgrounds. From left to right are Josephine Oaks, Anna Fitzpatrick, Margaret Lawson, Helen Toth, Bertha Miller, Mrs. Dunn, Ruth Suydam, Grace Shepperd, Hazel Shepperd, Anna Stout, and Dorothy Mathews. Kenneth Shepperd, born in 1921, remembers a wind-up Victrola playing while his sisters and their friends performed. (Courtesy Kenneth and Margaret Shepperd.)

It was a special event when the traveling grocery wagon came to town. Here Franklin residents are meeting in front of the old Capt. John Allen house, at the intersection of Allens Corner, Croton, and Franklin School Roads. They appear to have brought homegrown vegetables, fruit, and eggs with which to barter for various sundries. Lewis Henry Sanders, on the wagon, is handing a sack of flour to a local farmer. Sanders worked for M. Hall and Son in Flemington and went from hamlet to village with merchandise for sale or trade. The people are proudly posing for the camera with their newly acquired items around 1890. One wonders if these well-dressed farm families were asked to appear for a picture that could be used for promotional purposes. Signs on the pole proclaim "6 Miles to Flemington," "6 Miles to Everettstown," "1 Mile to Quakertown," "? Miles to Croton," and "Clothing for Big Men Sold at Nevius." (Courtesy Jeanette and Lewis Sanders.)

Oak Grove Grange No. 119, shown in the winter of 1916–1917, was organized in 1896, and the building was erected in 1898. Its membership peaked at over 100 in the mid-1950s, declined, and it was closed in 1987. The Grange movement existed nationwide from 1867 as a cooperative buying alliance for farmers. This Grange successfully petitioned for the county's first rural free delivery mail. (Courtesy Mary Bodine and family.)

The Grange was the first fraternal organization to admit women to full membership with men. It gave them the vote and advocated for women's suffrage 50 years before the 19th amendment. Pictured in June 1934, the distaff Oak Grove Grangers from left to right are Helen Burd, Anna Conover, Almeda Crane, and Ollie Burd. The man on the ladder is unidentified. (Courtesy Mary Bodine and family.)

ubadou - 1ˢᵗ Sgᵗ Paul Kuhl Co.A. J. Van Antwerp Co.E 1ˢᵗ Sg E.G. Budd Co.F 1ˢᵗ Sgᵗ 1ˢᵗ Sgᵗ W. E. Trimmer Co. G
lor Sergᵗ.)

1ˢᵗ Sgᵗ. H.R. Merrill Co. H. W. Johnson (Qr. Mr. Sergᵗ.) J.R McCauly (Actg Com't Sergᵗ.)

This detail of a portrait of the Union army's 1st Division, 6th Corps officers was taken in March 1864 by Weitfle and Wright Photographers. The man at right is 1st Sgt. William E. Trimmer, Company G, from Quakertown. On the opening day of the battle of Spotsylvania Court House in Virginia, Trimmer was in a group assigned to push out and penetrate the rebel line to assess their strength. Unsupported there, the troops were overwhelmed and had to retreat. He almost got back to his original line when he stopped to see how his men were doing. With his head exposed over tall grass, he was hit and killed at Laurel Hill on May 8, 1864, at age 24. The Union sustained 116 killed, 158 wounded, and 38 missing of the 429 who entered the battle. This was exceeded only once in numbers or percentages by any regiment in any battle of the Civil War. Trimmer is buried in Franklin's Locust Grove Cemetery. (Courtesy John W. Kuhl.)

World War I began in 1914. America joined in April 1917, and Franklin residents, like John R. Bodine, went to Europe to fight. Mothers hung a blue star in a window when a family member was in the war. A gold star meant the soldier had died in battle. Bodine came home safely. His son Richard W., born in 1924, married Mary Compton. (Courtesy Mary Bodine and family.)

Doughboy Linden Mathews and his young wife, Catherine Niece, pose at Fort Dix around 1917. Already a father before the war, Mathews came home and sired five more children. Catherine died in 1930, and Linden died in 1934 from illness related to being gassed in the trenches. In a true act of community spirit, relatives and neighbors raised the Mathews siblings to keep them near each other. (Courtesy Marjorie and Charles Mathews.)

Charles Carroll Wright, son of Harmon K. and Lillie Wright, was just 22 when this photograph was taken on October 14, 1917, at Camp Merritt, the largest embarkation camp in the United States during World War I. One of more than a million servicemen who passed through the site and sailed from Hoboken, he died from the flu one month after landing in France and is buried there. (Courtesy Mary Bodine and family.)

Young friends pose around 1943 after a Quakertown United Methodist Church service. Sailors Harold Verity (first row, left) and Bob Peterson (first row, right), the pastor's son, are home on furlough from World War II. Friends pleased to share their company again are (second row, from left to right) George Miller, Orville Barrick, and Lawrence Volk, all farmers the government would not call to war. Willis W. Vail's house is in the background. (Courtesy Volk family collection.)

Another young man home on leave from the U.S. Navy Armed Guard in June 1943 was John E. Wene, son of Earl and Laura Wene. John grew up on what is now Rutgers University's Snyder Research Farm on Locust Grove Road. The government called 119 Franklin men and women to service in World War II, almost 10 percent of the township population. (Courtesy Ted and Janice Wene Haas.)

Richard Porter was drafted into the U.S. Army in 1944 and is seen here while home on leave in 1945. Most of his service time was in the military police in occupied Japan. Discharged in 1946 and back home, he married Betty Jane Philhower from High Bridge and made a career in carpentry with Compton and Besch in Clinton. The couple had two daughters. (Courtesy Janice and Mike Parichuk.)

Quakertown resident Elizabeth Hanna Shepperd relaxes with her son Kenneth in 1942, just before he entered the Marine Corps. Kenneth served with the 1st Marine War Dog Platoon. He was stationed in the South Pacific and saw much action during World War II. Over the years, he has attended reunions with his war buddies and still resides in Franklin today. (Courtesy Kenneth and Margaret Shepperd.)

During World War II, Americans were asked to blacken automobile headlights so their vehicles would not be targets for enemy aircraft. Madeleine Marauda of Oak Grove and her daughter Alice show they complied with the government's request in this photograph from 1942. Willis W. Vail noted in his diary the day he "cleaned off the car headlights on account of release of the dim-out regulations." (Courtesy Marauda family.)

Marie Conover (left) and Dorothy Dalrymple scan the skies for World War II enemy aircraft in 1944 from a spotting station built on the Conover farm. Volunteers, who took classes and had a poster identifying airplanes, logged sightings and called a central command on a direct line to report a plane's location and direction. The building that once stood atop the tower was discovered on the property of Ted and Amy Poster in 2004, but its deteriorated state led to its dismantling. (Courtesy Virginia and Brevoort C. Conover.)

On June 20, 1943, during World War II, a World War I monument honoring men who served was dedicated at Franklin Township School. Lillian Wright (left, center) and Mrs. Alverter (right, center), both mothers of lost sons, unveiled the plaque. The men with them are John Tinnes (left) and Wallace Suydam. Emcee Frank Dalrymple introduced speakers Judge Gebhardt and Arthur Foran. Scouts gave flag salutes and taps. (Courtesy Mary Bodine and family.)

On February 26, 1938, the Hunterdon County Poultry Association held its annual banquet in the basement of the new Franklin Township School, the first large public function there since the building opened in the fall of 1937. Preparations began days earlier when turkeys and other fixings were dropped off at homes throughout the community. According to Willis W. Vail, 30 tables were set for 450 people, and it took 20 minutes for everyone to get down the stairs.

ANNUAL BANQUET
HUNTERDON CO. POULTRY ASSN.
AUDITORIUM HUNTERDON COUNTY
FEB 26, 1938

PHOTO
H. AVE
R.Y-1264

The audience sang songs between courses. Entertainment included tap dancing by an eight-year-old girl, short speeches by county officials and politicians, a magician, and then square dancing. Seven-year-old Brevoort C. Conover remembers dropping dry ice in the dish water and delighting when the water foamed up and scared the ladies organizing the meal. The school is still used for many community events. (Courtesy Volk family collection.)

Since the mid-1800s, groups of women have come together, making quilts as gifts or to raise funds for a good cause. At this *c.* 1896 quilting bee on the Volk farm, Laura Henry Volk is in the center holding her young son William Marvin. Many of the lighthearted women are displaying squares in the courthouse steps pattern, a variation of the log cabin pattern. (Courtesy Volk family collection.)

In rural communities such as Franklin, relatives and friends sat and shared gossip and wisdom while their fingers nimbly worked. In this 1920 photograph taken at the Wright farm, Mary Compton Bodine's aunts Ella Race (left) and Lizzie Hoppack are putting the finishing touches to the quilt on their laps. (Courtesy Mary Bodine and family.)

This photograph, dated February 7, 1935, is labeled, "Quakertown Needlecraft Club." Although the ladies are not displaying their stitchery projects, they are pictured from left to right as (first row) Thisbe Leaver, Anna Stout Cullen, Jean Banghart, and Irma Suydam; (second row) Bertha Miller, Hannah Emery, Mildred Dissler (with arm on Leaver's shoulder), Ruth Suydam, Helen Smith, and Hazel Shepperd. (Courtesy Charles W. Eichlin.)

Brothers David T. and Brevoort W. Conover grew up on a farm in Cherryville loving baseball. Since Franklin had no teams in the 1890s, they played for Clinton and made fine battery mates. David pitched and Brevoort caught. It was a 4- to 5-mile ride by horse and buggy to get to the playing field. (Courtesy Virginia and Brevoort C. Conover.)

Teenaged Quakertown baseball teammates Orville Barrick (left) and Lawrence Volk are shown around 1939. Barrick's interest in baseball waned, but Volk, a crackerjack first baseman, continued to play. He was even invited to try out for the Philadelphia Athletics, without success. World War II broke up the Quakertown team. Volk played a while for Flemington but gave up the sport for growing family responsibilities. (Courtesy Volk family collection.)

If one asked these young boys, who are happily diving off a bridge abutment into the South Branch of the Raritan River along the Old River Road, they would say that pools are for sissies. Nationally renowned photographer Walter Chandoha caught his two sons, Enrico and Samuel, and an unidentified neighbor enjoying the water in the mid-1960s—even if one is headed for a belly flop. (Photograph by Walter Chandoha.)

The Lockatong Swim Club pool was behind the Independent Order of Odd Fellows's building in Quakertown and was active less than a decade. Members paid a one-time fee of $250. Elizabeth Braidwood (center), at age 10, enjoyed the pool in 1969 with two other members. Just a few years later, the Odd Fellows sold the building. It was made into apartments and the pool removed. (Courtesy Braidwood family.)

After returning to his Quakertown ancestral home in the 1920s, Willis W. Vail saw that many boys were idle and up to shenanigans. He started mentoring them, and his Quakertown Chums club evolved into the Franklin Township's first Boy Scout troop (No. 108) in 1928. In this c. 1930 photograph, Vail (left) enjoys a snack in the woods with Fred Polascek (center) and Albert Leaver. (Courtesy Fred and Jean Polascek.)

In June 1935, members of troop 108 pose for Vail's camera during a nine-day camping trip. From left to right are Harold Mathews, Albert Leaver, Allen Trout, Anatoly Mishuk, and Fred Polascek. The group enjoyed swimming, rowing, hiking, and "doggie roasts." Polascek still speaks highly of Vail and how he taught them, by example, to become good citizens of Franklin Township. (Courtesy Fred and Jean Polacsek.)

Vail was so loved that on his 79th birthday in 1947, 300 people attended a surprise dinner honoring him. Many of Vail's former Scouts, now community leaders themselves, spoke about their mentor. Vail died on August 4, 1951. This early-1950s photograph shows Boy Scout Troop No. 108 parading by the Friends meetinghouse following a dedication service held to install a plaque at his graveside. (Courtesy Quakertown Friends Meeting.)

James Foran got Troop 108 reinstituted in 2001. Rebuilding a Capoolong Trail bridge are, from left to right, (first row) Scott Sakos, Kenny Dahler, Lucas Michael, Matt Michael, Case Hoff, John Greczylo Jr., Justine Dagnall, Jeff Becker, Tommy Buch, John Scarpa, and James "J. D." Foran; (second row) unidentified, Barry Michael, Kelly Hoff, John Greczylo Sr., John Perkins, Dr. Raymond Buch, and Foran. Like Willis Vail before him, Foran teaches Scouts qualities to last a lifetime. (Courtesy Franklin Township Troop 108.)

Franklin's kindergarten teacher Elsie VanWyck leads a parade through Cherryville in the 1950s to celebrate bible school graduation at the Baptist church, identified by the steeple over her shoulder. The children wore festive headdresses; some dads drove tractors. VanWyck's husband, LaRee, decorated his tractor to look like a fish and could make it spew water. Everyone paraded three-tenths of a mile to Sabo Lane and back. (Courtesy LaRee VanWyck.)

Jamming on the farmhouse porch in the 1930s was popular with the Schultz family and their friends. Schultz brothers John (left, with mandolin) and Chester (with banjo) sit with Clara Burns from New York City (with accordion) and Schultz cousin Adolph Schillberg (with guitar). Chester had the ability to play both chords and melody at the same time to sound like two banjoes. (Courtesy Schultz family.)

James and Rae Braidwood were both active with the Girl Scouts. Rae led the local troop in Cherryville and also helped with the Rolling Hills Girl Scout canoe program. James took this picture in 1966 of the canoeing group on the South Branch of the Raritan River. The parents' efforts must have been effective, since their daughter Elizabeth Braidwood loves canoeing to this day. (Courtesy Braidwood family.)

A face-painted Elizabeth Braidwood of Cherryville, age eight, is having fun at the Hunterdon County Fair in Flemington in 1967. The outing was part of a YMCA Indian Guide program aimed at fostering companionship and understanding between fathers and daughters. Elizabeth remembers having a great day with her dad and sitting in the bleachers with him to watch the automobile races. (Courtesy Braidwood family.)

Halloween celebrations reached a peak in the second and third decades of the 20th century. Since rural farms were far apart in Franklin, parades and parties were held at schoolhouses or community buildings. Anna Natalie Miller, age 19, is dressed in her fashionable Halloween costume in preparation for the masquerade party hosted by the Patriotic Order of Sons of America in a Quakertown building owned by the Odd Fellows. There are a few inches of snow at her feet on this sunny October 31, 1925, afternoon. Willis W. Vail noted in his diary that it started to snow at 7:30 p.m. on October 30 and there was about 2 inches on the ground at night. The day of the masquerade, temperatures were 25 degrees in the morning and 42 degrees at noon. Vail, at age 57, went to the party in costume and wrote, "I do not think anyone recognized me, and I left at the time unmasking was in order." (Courtesy Virginia and Brevoort C. Conover.)

During those early years of the 20th century, children made costumes from scratch with the aid of patterns, as detailed in magazines and books of the day. Here Fannie Compton (left) and her sister Mary show off their festive homemade attire in this photograph taken around 1929. (Courtesy Mary Bodine and family.)

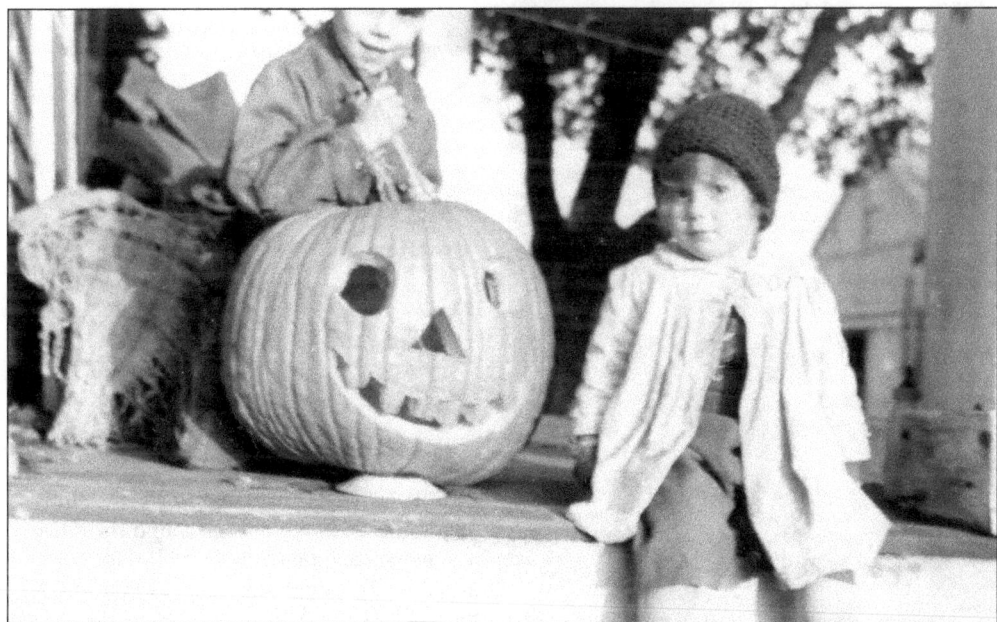

The Depression hit Franklin in the 1930s, and celebrations were less ostentatious than in earlier years. World War II and the rationing of goods put a halt to Halloween altogether. The holiday returned in earnest when baby boomers reached trick-or-treating age in the early 1950s. James (left) and Judith Passerello carve their jack-o'-lantern for the 1956 Halloween season. (Courtesy James and Mary Passerello and Judith Winfield.)

Springhill Road has a tradition of friendliness among its residents and numerous hills that call to youngsters after a snow. These four neighborhood children spent a chilly afternoon (just look at that sky) in the mid-1960s trudging uphill with their big saucers to get the thrill of the fast ride back down. Walter Chandoha, who lives on the road, was there to record the fun. (Photograph by Walter Chandoha.)

Orville Barrick (in the light jacket) helps 1960s guests off a hayride around the dairy and grain farm he owned and ran for over 50 years on Wolverton Road. A Franklin native, he was a leader in many farming awareness and advocacy groups, as well as civic organizations. He served on the township committee from 1961 through 1972 and was mayor three times. (Photograph by Walter Chandoha.)

Six families who met monthly to play the card game 500 also enjoyed an annual picnic. Here at Audrey and Orville Barrick's 23-room Victorian mansion in 1963 are, from left to right, LouAnn Miller (Adams), Marian Miller, Linda Barrick (Squires), Bob Miller, Libby Dalrymple, Keith Vanderbilt, Bob Reed, Ruth Reed, Charles Reed, Nancy and Don Dalrymple, Don Barrick, Lynda Rozzo, Danny Reed, Larry Vanderbilt, George Miller, and Harry Vanderbilt. (Courtesy Orville Barrick family.)

From left to right, township committee members Charles Mathews, Charles Patkochis, and Mayor August Knispel dressed in 1776 attire to celebrate the nation's bicentennial anniversary. Ceremonies included planting red oak liberty trees donated by township nurseryman Robert Fox at the Franklin Township School in Quakertown and the municipal building in Sidney. The Easy Riders horse club of Pittstown, also costumed, appeared at both sites. (Photograph by Walter Chandoha.)

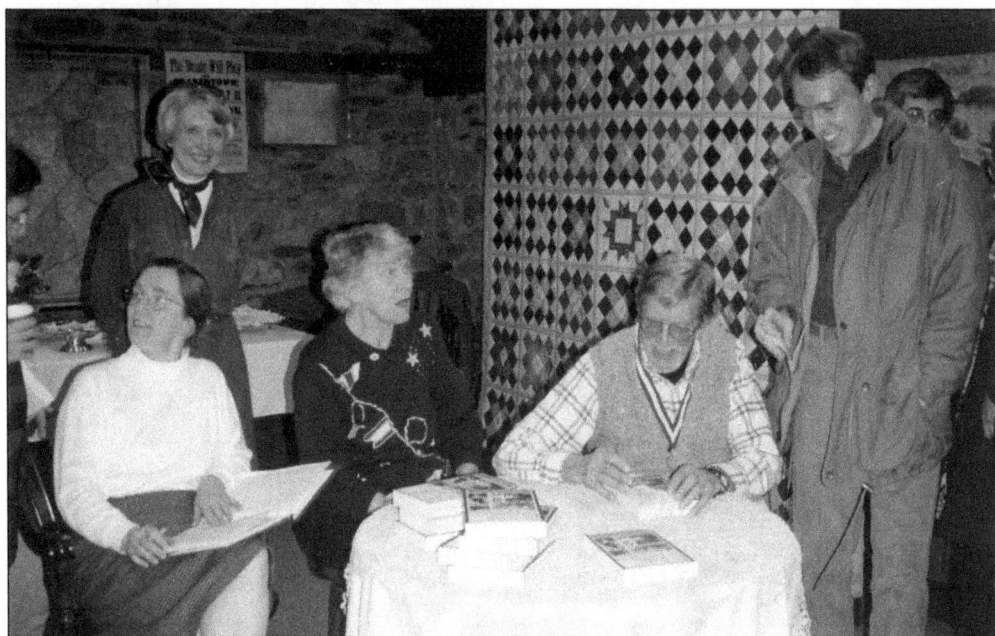

A major event for Franklin's 1995 sesquicentennial celebration was the signing of *Facts and Fantasies of Franklin,* a 418-page history with photographs, maps, and the 1850 census by longtime township historian J. Edward Stout. From left to right are Carolyn Millhiser, Lora Jones (standing), Evelyn Lawson, Stout, and his son Joey Stout. The quilt was made by a Stout family member. (Courtesy Franklin Archives.)

Franklin residents capped a June 3, 1995, sesquicentennial celebratory afternoon parade through Quakertown with a square dance for all ages that evening at a Rutgers research farm barn. More than a promenade and a do-si-do to lively music, there was real shortcake made by Quakertown resident Pat Porter that was topped with real cream and the sweetest, just-picked strawberries found in Franklin. (Courtesy Franklin Archives.)

Putting fire trucks in parades, like this one seen during Franklin's 1995 sesquicentennial event, is an old New Jersey tradition. The truck pictured is owned by the all-volunteer Quakertown Fire Company, which was founded in 1914 and reorganized in 1951. Fire companies from other communities also participated, along with rescue squads, antique cars, farm vehicles, and a float made by Franklin students. (Courtesy Franklin Archives.)

In 2009, Rural Awareness asked township students to interview senior residents about life here before 1950. Pictured from left to right, the scholar award winners in front of a historical 1837 one-room schoolhouse are Rachel Schultz, Hallie Mathews, Brendan Flanigan (the grand champion), Tyler Marcantuono, Jessen Haug, Courtney Schwar, and Anna Piparo. These children and their classmates are the future of Franklin's beautiful rural community. (Photograph by Marty Campanelli.)

BIBLIOGRAPHY

Brecknell, Ursula. *National Register of Historic Places, Quakertown and Pittstown District submission 1987.* Hunterdon County, NJ: Rural Awareness, Inc., 1987.

Campanelli, Dan and Marty Campanelli. *Did the British Troops Occupy Quakertown, New Jersey During the Revolutionary War?* Hunterdon County, NJ: self-published, 2007.

Hitchcock, Frederick H. *The Letters of Moore Furman.* New Jersey Society of the Colonial Dames of America, 1912.

Hunterdon County Cultural and Heritage Commission. *The First 275 Years of Hunterdon County 1714–1989.* Hunterdon County, NJ: Hunterdon County Cultural and Heritage Commission, 1989.

Jones, Lora. "A History of Franklin Township," Harvest Home Tour brochure. Hunterdon County, NJ: Rural Awareness, Inc., 2008.

———. "A Self-Guided Walking Tour of Historic Quakertown," Harvest Home Tour brochure. Hunterdon County, NJ: Rural Awareness, Inc., 2008.

Lequear, John W. *Traditions of Hunterdon, Traditions of Our Ancestors.* Flemington, NJ: D. H. Moreau, 1957.

McCormick, Richard P. *New Jersey From Colony to State 1609–1789.* New Brunswick, NJ: Rutgers University Press, 1964.

Moore, James W. *Records of the Kingwood Monthly Meeting of Friends, Hunterdon County New Jersey.* Flemington, NJ: H. E. Deats, 1900.

Schmidt, Hubert G. *Rural Hunterdon—An Agricultural History.* New Brunswick, NJ: Rutgers University Press, 1945.

Snell, James P. *History of Hunterdon and Somerset Counties, New Jersey, with Illustrations and Biographical Sketches of its Prominent Men and Pioneers.* Philadelphia: Everts and Peck, 1881.

Stout, J. E. *Facts and Fantasies of Franklin.* Hunterdon County, NJ: Franklin Township Committee, 1995.

Township of Franklin Tercentenary Celebration, October 17, 1964. Hunterdon County, NJ: Township Committee and Board of Education, 1964.

Wacker, Peter O. *The Musconetcong Valley of New Jersey.* New Brunswick, NJ: Rutgers University Press, 1968.

ABOUT RURAL AWARENESS, INC.

"Hay Day" © Dan Campanelli

Rural Awareness, Inc.

Rural Awareness is a nonprofit organization formed in 1982 by citizens interested in the past, present, and future of Franklin Township, Hunterdon County, as a rural and agricultural community. Its objective is to preserve the quality of life in Franklin by fostering community pride through civic involvement. Its projects promote the preservation of the unique and historic character of artifacts, structures, and scenic landscapes. The organization annually honors a Franklin resident who exemplifies outstanding practices of conservation, agriculture, or community service with the Hiram Deats Award. Rural Awareness scholar awards are given to Franklin students whose essays best highlight the importance of the community's rural character and its effects on lifestyle and economy. Rural Awareness, Inc., raises funds for civic projects by hosting concerts and conducting tours of historic houses in Franklin. It also sells a 17-minute DVD, *Passing Glances*, of Franklin's first 150 years. Funds have been used to list Quakertown and Pittstown as historic districts on the New Jersey state and national registers, to host candidates' nights for municipal and board of education elections, and to support the food pantry at the Quakertown United Methodist Church. A project to replace the foundation of an 1837 one-room schoolhouse was completed with the generous help of Stephen and Michael Mergentime, Franklin residents who own a specialty engineering and construction company. Visit the Web site at www.ruralawareness.org for a list of farms that sell directly to consumers and to see a photographic gallery showing the beauty and character of Franklin. Note also the large historic Lenape Indian mortar that was found and put on display. August Knispel, founding member and lifelong Franklin promoter, is Rural Awareness, Inc.'s, president-for-life. The organization meets once monthly and has no dues. All who are interested in supporting its goals are invited to join in.

127

Visit us at
arcadiapublishing.com

···

www.ingramcontent.com/pod-product-compliance
Lightning Source LLC
Chambersburg PA
CBHW050623110426
42813CB00007B/1703